Testimoni.

WHEN HAL SIMONSON TOOK OVER OUR ACCOUNT the first thing he did was learn more about us as a family, what our interests were, what our concerns were and what our expectations were, both short-term and long-term. Hal assessed our financial position and then worked with us to develop a long-term financial plan that considered our lifestyle, our children's education and our retirement. We have a strong relationship, and we are confident our plan is achieving our long-term goals with an advisor who cares.

- Fern and David, Sherwood Park

WE HAVE FELT CONFIDENT IN THE ADVICE that Hal has provided for us in our financial undertakings and appreciate his attention to detail. The frequent meetings that we have had and the written analysis that he has provided for us have allowed us to plan for our future retirement while maintaining a comfortable financial standard of living. Hal has provided excellent service not only for Gerry and me but also for my parents and our children.

- Cindy and Gerry, St. Albert

HAL "PUSHES" INFORMATION AND RECOMMENDATIONS, WHICH IS invaluable in a busy time and world when thinking about the market is the last priority on my mind. He has provided written plans and analyses, and has been a cornerstone in continuity by keeping in contact with me several times a year, regardless of the state of the markets.

- Dr. R.C.A., Edmonton

How to Give Like a Billionaire

WHEN YOU'RE NOT A BILLIONAIRE

HAL SIMONSON

HOW TO GIVE LIKE A BILLIONAIRE
When You're Not a Billionaire

Copyright © Hal Simonson, 2025

Published by Hal Simonson, Edmonton, Canada

ISBN:
Paperback   978-1-77354-629-2
    ebook   978-1-77354-631-5

Publication assistance and digital printing in Canada by

PUBLISHING
PageMaster.ca

Dedication

For my mother, Leanne, my first teacher
of all things generous and loving.

Contents

Preface

SINCE PUTTING MYSELF THROUGH POST-SECONDARY SCHOOL VIA the Regular Officer Training Program (military university) and serving three years as an army platoon commander, I've operated a financial planning practice with a pioneering Canadian financial firm. For over two and a half decades now, with the help of my firm and their leading-edge financial planning software, I've helped hundreds of families plan for and reach a financially secure retirement. My team often takes delight in working with multiple client family generations (our current record is four at a time).

In 2020 and 2021, while much of the world was suffering in so many ways, I spent a lot of time reflecting on how fortunate I and those I care about were. My career is enjoyable and rewarding, and my clients are wonderful people who I often enjoy spending time with socially. However, I was aware that they too were among the most fortunate people on the planet, simply by virtue of being Canadians with above average wealth. With that in mind, I decided to expand our scope of work to include a focus on tax efficient estate planning and charitable giving. We have an obligation to take advantage of our good fortune and give back. Plus, if we can pay less taxes along the way, even better!

Our mission is to make the world a better place through values based financial planning, sustainable investing, and philanthropic planning

My hope in writing this book is that it will increase awareness of the different tools and strategies available to Canadians who are interested in sharing their good fortune. While a handful of books/technical manuals exist, they are written for advisors like me, or other professionals such as accountants and lawyers. I have not been able to find anything written for working or retired Canadians outside the financial services industry. To that end I've received permission from several of our clients who have used these strategies in real life and were very happy to permit me to include their words in this book. I hope this will make the content more relatable. To those clients I extend my heartfelt gratitude.

A shout out to my business partner and good friend Scott Skjei

While over 95% of the words on these pages are mine, Scott is the team Tax Nerd, a title he holds with great joy. Scott was an essential sounding board from the minute I considered writing the book. He wrote the first draft of the chapter on tax rules around corporate donations, and has proofread everything you'll see in this book, especially any tax related math. He's also a great friend.

And the rest of Simonson Team Private Wealth Management

Many thanks to Devon, a fully licensed advisor on the team who also serves as the practice manager. She's a better mentee than a mentor could ever hope for, and has taught me more than I've taught her. My beloved wife Sarah is the executive assistant for the team, and always ready to bring a dose of adult supervision to the more hairbrained of my and Scott's ideas. Both ladies proofread and gave excellent feedback on the first draft of this book.

What this book is:

- A source of information.
- An insight into charitable giving strategies used by average Canadians in real life.
- As accurate as possible with respect to legislation and tax rates at time of writing.
- Something to share with friends and family who may feel the same about charitable giving and making the world a better place. Give them this book when you are finished, or even better, send an email to book@halsimonson.ca and I'll send a copy or three to anyone and everyone you wish.

What this book is not:

- Advice: the content between these covers is for informational purposes, with the hope that when you're ready to get personal advice you'll contact Simonson Team Private Wealth Management or take this book to your existing financial advisory team. Everyone deserves a complete financial analysis before making any type of major money decision. There is a myriad of financial planning designations in Canada. The best financial planning teams for philanthropic work will include one or more advisors with these designations:
  - CERTIFIED FINANCIAL PLANNER (CFP®): this should be the absolute minimum requirement you look for when you need personal financial advice,
  - Master Financial Advisor – Philanthropy (MFA-P™): a designation focussed on charitable planning strategies,

- ○ Chartered Life Underwriter (CLU®) – Canada's premier wealth transfer and estate planning designation, and
- ○ Trust and Estate Practitioner (TEP) – The TEP designation demonstrates that the advisor has an advanced understanding of the trust and estates field and that they take a proactive approach to being at the forefront of the latest developments in the industry.

Note that working with a financial advisor does not mean you should not engage other professionals, particularly accountants and lawyers, in the appropriate situations. In fact, our best work as financial advisors is done when we're in close communication and cooperation with our client's other professional advisors.

- • Perfectly accurate: almost certainly one or several governments in the country will change something as soon as this book is sent to print:
  - ○ Each calendar year that passes will, at a minimum, see indexation of the tax brackets.
  - ○ During the course of authoring this book:
    - » two government budget cycles took place.
    - » the capital gains inclusion rate has changed for large ($250,000+) individual gains and incorporated entities.
    - » broad changes were made to Alternative Minimum Tax (AMT) legislation by CRA.
    - » specific elements of the changes to the AMT legislation had potential negative impacts on philanthropic planning.
  - ○ Often between budget announcement and enshrinement in legislation, the proposed changes are subject to modification.

- Suffice it to say that tax planning has ever moving targets and getting advice from a professional who works hard to stay up to date is essential.

- A for-profit venture: I did not author this book to make money from selling it. It's not even an "all profits will be donated to charity" type of endeavor. Copies of this book will be distributed by my team free of charge, and if you happened to purchase it via an online platform then it was priced only enough to recoup any distribution costs incurred.

I've tried to make it more readable by simplifying a few things:

- Most numbers in this book are rounded to even numbers. The difference between $12,432 and $12,500, or $1,312,984 and $1.3M is not material in the examples listed. When you are ready to go down this path, my team would be happy to give you precise numbers as part of a personal analysis and philanthropic plan.

- I have used the term *executor* when referring to the person you appoint in your will to settle your affairs after you pass away. Some jurisdictions have moved to *trustee, personal representative,* or *estate administrator,* but I'm confident everyone understands the term executor. There are many different situations where we could encounter the terms administrator, representative or trustee in roles not related to an estate.

- When a Donor Advised Fund is projected to earn a certain rate of return as a long-term average, we do the math as if that is the exact rate of return each year. Of course, investment returns are always higher or lower than average in any given year, however using a simple long-term average gives us a strong working sense of the potential long-term results.

- Generally, in the text when you see the term 'gross' as in 'gross amount' or 'gross income', we're using that to mean before taxes are paid. The term 'net' refers to after tax amounts.

The chapters in this book are all prefaced in one of these ways:

- Background: these chapters contain background information on charitable planning and the tax rules related to donations. As this is not an academic publication, your author has not cited a reference for every single piece of information (most of which come from the Government of Canada website and are readily searchable online) though there are some references for lesser know facts about giving.
- Case Study: these chapters contain examples of giving strategies that are generic and available to most Canadians.
- Giving in Real Life: these chapters are real life stories about Canadians who have already started giving like billionaires. These stories have been anonymized to the extent requested by the philanthropists involved.
- Advanced: these chapters are grouped towards the back of the book. Feel free to skip these chapters if a glance at the title indicates that the situation discussed does not apply to you.

Terminology that will come up frequently in the pages to come:

Canada Revenue Agency (CRA) – the federal government department that collects taxes on behalf of the Government of Canada, and all provinces and territories except Quebec.

Donor Advised Fund (DAF) - the account held at a Parent Foundation "advised" by the donor (you!).

Parent Foundation (PF) – the term I use for the officially incorporated charitable foundation that handles all the administration for the Donor Advised Funds it manages on behalf of clients.

Beneficiary Charity (BC) – the term I use for a registered charity that is the beneficiary of the annual disbursements from a Donor Advised Fund.

Disclosure

This book is not a source of customized personal financial advice. No client-advisor relationship is formed by the distribution of this book.

The intent of the book is to raise awareness of the various ways in which it is possible to donate with a legacy in mind. The Reader is encouraged to take their interest in charitable giving, along with a basic understanding of the concepts described within, to a philanthropic planning professional in order to receive bespoke advice and service.

Rates of return noted in the examples that follow are deemed by the author to be reasonable for illustration purposes but cannot be assured or guaranteed in any way.

1

How Billionaires Give

"Is the rich world aware of how four billion of the six billion live? If we were aware, we would want to help out, we'd want to get involved." – Bill Gates

THE FIRST STEP ON THE JOURNEY TO giving like billionaires is learning how billionaires give, and how they don't give. Billionaires tend towards planned, strategic giving. They seldom donate based on:

- headline news about a recent natural disaster,
- participating in a "fun event" such as a walkathon or charity auction,
- advertising or social media campaigns,
- celebrity endorsements, or
- workplace campaigns that include implicit and explicit pressure from peers and leaders.

It's important to note that while those types of donations can be valuable, it's also essential to consider giving on a planned basis to ensure that charities have a consistent source of funding throughout the year. Many of the charities that do the best day to day work are not glamorous, and we don't see them in headlines. Examples include food banks, family violence centres, global health initiatives, or education programs.

It's fair to assume that everyone in the world who is a billionaire today came to that wealth via themself or a close family member having significant business success, so we should not be surprised that billionaires run their philanthropic activities as businesses. They:

- incorporate an entity to manage the giving,
- develop a charter or mission statement to focus the organization,
- hire staff to operate the organization, and
- recruit a board of directors to guide the organization towards the fulfilment of that charter.

What are those entities called? Foundations. You've probably heard of some of them: The Rockefeller Foundation and the Ford Foundation were created in 1913 and 1936 respectively, by wealthy businesspeople inspired to share their good fortune in the hope of making the world a better place. The Mastercard Foundation, headquartered in Toronto, was formed in 2006 when Mastercard Incorporated became a publicly traded company. As part of that transition from private to public company, Mastercard donated 13.5 million shares worth about US$600 million to the new charitable foundation[1].

This idea is not as new as the 20th century, it's much older than that. The City Bridge Foundation in London, England, traces its origins back to 1282 when it was established to maintain London

---

1   Mastercard Foundation - Wikipedia

Bridge. Eventually it expanded to maintain (and occasionally replace) other bridges in the city, and by the 1990s had accumulated such a large real estate portfolio that its income exceeded the cost of maintaining the bridges. It now disburses surplus income for other charitable purposes in the Greater London area[2].

The most famous foundation in the world is probably the Bill & Melinda Gates Foundation. Including a $20 billion USD donation in 2022, the Gates have donated over US$59 billion to the foundation since inception, bolstered by another US$35.7 billion from Warren Buffett[3].

Foundations are not the type of charitable organization to perform the work we imagine when we think of charities in action; foundations are not the "boots on the ground". Rather, foundations direct money from their financial endowments to charities on an ongoing basis, according to their charter. The Gates Foundation, for example, has distributed US$71.4 billion since inception, through the end of 2022, including US$7 billion in the year 2022, while still maintaining an endowment reserve fund worth US$67 billion at the end of that year[4].

Such massive endeavours undoubtably make the world a better place. The Gates Foundation alone is credited with saving over 50,000,000 lives through it's Global Health Division, via medicine, nutritional supplements, vaccinations, and malaria nets distributed to impoverished communities around the world[5]. FIFTY MILLION!

But what if you're not a billionaire? How do you make a difference? As you'll see in the next chapter, it's all a matter of scale.

---

2   City Bridge Foundation - Wikipedia
3   Foundation Fact Sheet (At A Glance) | Bill & Melinda Gates Foundation website
4   Foundation Fact Sheet (At A Glance) | Bill & Melinda Gates Foundation website
5   Bill Gates on How the Global Fund Saves Millions of Lives | Bill & Melinda Gates Foundation website

2

But I'm not a Billionaire, How Can I Make a Difference?

"The smallest act of charity can ignite a fire of hope." – Leo Evans

MOST OF US DON'T HAVE THE CHARITABLE giving budget of a software billionaire but even small gifts matter, especially to the recipients. According to CharityIntelligence.ca website's list of the Top 10 Impact Charities of 2022, there are many ways to make an impact in your community for less than $100:

- Donate to a local food bank: A donation of $25 can provide a family of four with a week's worth of groceries.
- Support a homeless shelter: A donation of $50 can provide a homeless person with a hot meal, a shower, and a warm bed for the night.
- Contribute to a children's hospital: A donation of $75 can provide a child with a toy or a book to help them feel more comfortable during their stay.

- Donate to a disaster relief fund: A donation of $25 can provide a family with clean water for a week after a natural disaster.
- Support a local animal shelter: A donation of $50 can provide a shelter animal with food, toys, and medical care.
- Donate to a women's shelter: A donation of $25 can provide a woman with a safe place to sleep for a night.
- Support a community center: A donation of $50 can help fund after-school programs for children.
- Donate to a local library: A donation of $25 can help fund new books and other resources for the community.

Here are ten ways to make a charitable impact internationally with a donation of $100 or less[6]:

- Donate to Against Malaria Foundation: A donation of $100 can provide 20 mosquito nets to protect people from malaria.
- Support Canadian Foodgrains Bank: A donation of $75 can provide a family with enough food to last for a month.
- Contribute to The Citizen's Foundation: A donation of $50 can provide a child with a year's worth of education.
- Donate to Doctors Without Borders: A donation of $100 can provide medical care to 10 people in need.
- Support Effect Hope: A donation of $75 can provide treatment for 5 people suffering from leprosy.
- Contribute to Farm Radio International: A donation of $50 can provide a farmer with access to agricultural information and resources.
- Donate to Lifewater Canada: A donation of $100 can provide clean water to 10 people for a year.

---

6   Source: Top 10 International Impact Charities 2022 - Charity Intelligence Canada

- Support Mennonite Central Committee Canada: A donation of $75 can provide a family with a month's worth of food and supplies.
- Contribute to Operation Eyesight Universal: A donation of $50 can provide eye care to 5 people in need.
- Donate to World Vision - A donation of $100 can provide a family with a goat, which can provide milk and income for years to come.

While the above items do not have the grandiosity of a multi-million-dollar donation, they do have a real impact. Twenty mosquito nets can save one or more people from malaria, clean water for a year can keep a family from getting cholera, and a year of education can start a budding young scientist on the path to a future world-changing breakthrough.

While billionaires create private foundations with high profile boards of directors and lots of publicity, the rest of us can create our own mini foundations by piggybacking on a public foundation. We can name our mini foundations, create our own informal board of directors, and provide long term financial support to the causes we care about.

These mini foundations are called Donor Advised Funds (DAFs), a type of charitable account that exists within a larger Parent Foundation (PF). In the next chapter we'll learn more about how a Donor Advised Fund operates.

3
Background

But I'm Not a Billionaire, How Can I Have a Foundation?

"We're all in this together. Each and every one of us can make a difference by giving back." – Beyoncé

YOU DON'T NEED HAVE TO HAVE A 10-figure bank account balance to create a charitable entity that supports the causes important to you on an ongoing basis. Although it's widely accepted that creating a private foundation is not practical if you plan to donate less than $5,000,000[7] (because of the overhead costs) there is an alternative for the rest of us, the Donor Advised Fund (DAF).

It's best to think of a DAF as an account held through an established foundation, which we'll call the Parent Foundation (PF). The PF can be a community foundation, a public foundation administered by a financial institution, or a similar entity offered by another (often faith based) organization. The PF is always a charity

---

7   This amount could be much higher if the PF in question will negotiate lower administration fees for larger DAFs.

registered with CRA and will issue charitable donation receipts for your contributions.

The Parent Foundation does all the hard work: keeping the books, fulfilling legal and reporting requirements, issuing tax receipts, and delivering the money to the Beneficiary Charities (BCs). The Donor (you!) gives advice on what charities to distribute the money to, names the DAF, and makes the donations to the DAF, maybe consulting with other friends or family who share a similar value set – your own board of directors!

Creating a Donor Advised Fund is a fairly straightforward process. With the help of a qualified financial advisor, you'll have to complete some new account paperwork, similar to any other investment account you've ever opened.

This paperwork will specify:

- The donor/account holder,
- The joint account holder if applicable,
- The successor account holder – the one who will become the account holder upon the death of the initial account holder(s) – if applicable,
- The name you've chosen for the DAF,
- The initial list of Beneficiary Charities,
- Instructions on how to invest the DAF's endowment funds, and
- Instructions on what time of year to make the charitable distributions, and what percentage of the DAF to disburse annually (typically 5%).

Then you'll make your initial donation to your Donor Advised Fund, either by cash, or with one of the other strategies you'll learn about in this book. Often over the course of your giving journey you'll use several of the strategies available to you, making gifts of cash, investments, and maybe insurance.

You'll recall from the chapter on *How Billionaires Give* that a foundation is not the charitable organization that does the actual charitable work. Foundations typically maintain a pool of investments and use money from investment earnings to distribute to the BCs on an annual basis.

The Parent Foundation is itself a charitable entity, and donations we make to the PF are receipted the same as if we donated directly to a Beneficiary Charity. Once we make the donation the money belongs to the Foundation, and the donor no longer has direct control over the funds. However, remember that we've created a Donor **Advised** Fund. The Board of Directors for the PF will take advice from the donors on how to manage the investments, how to distribute the money to the BCs, and even change the BCs when we advise them to do so.

It's important to note that we do not get another charitable donation receipt when our DAF distributes money to a Beneficiary Charity. Once we've made the initial donation to our DAF, the money is in the charitable sphere. Moving money from one charitable organization (the DAF account within the PF) to another (the BC) is not a new charitable donation, just as transferring assets from one RRSP to another is not a new RRSP contribution.

Aside from farming out all the administrative chores, another benefit of a Donor Advised Find is that the Parent Foundation places a layer between you and the Beneficiary charity. One of your options when you create a DAF is to have the PF distribute the annual donations anonymously, to share only the name of the DAF, or to share your name and address with the Beneficiary charity. You get to control the level of exposure you and your DAF get.

As you'll read soon in the chapter about the *B Family Charitable Fund*, keeping control of your contact information can save you from a lot of unwanted phone and mail solicitations, while allowing you to focus on the causes you are most passionate about.

4

Carrying on the Family Name: The B Family Charitable Fund

"We make a living by what we get. We make a life by what we give." – Winston Churchill

Dr. and Mrs. B. agreed to let me tell their story for this book but asked to remain anonymous. They have been clients of my firm since the 1990s and Dr. B. only fully retired in the last decade, after working into his early 70s. Mrs. B. managed the household, raised their daughter and son, and has always tended a fantastic garden.

A few years ago, Dr. and Mrs. B. lost their son unexpectedly. As it happened, at that time we were in the middle of revising their estate plan to account for the fact that their daughter has two children while their son had none. After losing their son we commenced a conversation about starting a family legacy fund, for several reasons:

- Dr. and Mrs. B. had long supported several charitable causes. Dr. B.'s mother "was a generous sort" who had impressed upon him the value of giving back when he was a young man.

- We projected that their estate would be quite substantial, much more than their daughter (who was already financially secure) could ever use in her lifetime, especially given that she was now the sole surviving child.
- The B family name was not going to continue past Dr. and Mrs. B.'s passing, given that their daughter and grandsons (and three great-grandchildren) had a different family name.

Dr. B. is a doctor of the science Ph.D. sort. He had worked for some resource companies in the past and had several hundred thousand dollars of publicly traded stock that had only cost him a fraction of that to purchase when he was participating in the employee stock plans.

Once we decided to create the B. Family Charitable Fund, we used these stocks as the initial donation to set up the Donor Advised Fund. Dr. and Mrs. B.'s initial donation was approximately $200,000 in stock upon which there was a $180,000 capital gain. By making the in-kind stock donation they were able to avoid the inclusion of $90,000 of taxable income on that year's tax returns (saving about $40,000 in income tax – see the chapter *Donations of Publicly Traded Securities*) and received charitable donation credits of $100,000. The net result was the creation of a family legacy fund with $200,000 as the initial balance (and therefore the 5% annual donations started at $10,000) while only reducing their substantial after-tax net worth by $60,000.

As mentioned, Dr. and Mrs. B. had a long history of charitable giving, donating several thousands of dollars each year to many charities in amounts ranging from $100-$500 dollars. One of the unfortunate side effects of this was that they came to be on the contact list for many charities, and at the worst point were receiving solicitations at the rate of more than one phone call per day and approximately 100 pieces of mail per month. Once we created the B Family Charitable Fund, my staff helped Dr. and Mrs. B. sent letters to all the charities that had been soliciting them, asking that they not be contacted in the future. This resulted in a greater than 90% decrease in the mail solicitations Dr. and Mrs. B. receive.

While preferring to remain anonymous, Dr. and Mrs. B. did agree to be interviewed for this book. Here are some snippets from that conversation:

How have your motivations or perspectives on charitable giving evolved over the years? *Our choice of charities has changed over time because of personal experience, particularly illnesses that impacted family members later in life.*

How did you choose what charitable organizations or causes to support, and what criteria do you consider when making these decisions? *Our primary criteria are helping family, friends, and our community. For example, we support the University of Alberta Hospital where Dr. B. was treated after suffering serious burns from a gas well explosion. Similarly, we donate to research to cure Parkinson's Disease which afflicted Mrs. B.'s younger brother.*

Do you involve your family or close associates in your philanthropic activities? *We discussed our intent to undertake creating the charitable fund with our daughter and her husband. She will take over the fund after we pass, and we're pleased that it will pass down through further generations over time. Before his passing our son supported STARS (the Shock Trauma Air Rescue Service) so we've included that in his memory.*

What type of impact do you hope to achieve through your philanthropic efforts? *Our impact is small, but if everyone did it the world would be a magnificent place.*

What advice would you offer to others who are considering making substantial charitable donations, especially if they want to make a meaningful impact? *Just do it! It won't hurt, and it might even make you feel good.*

The B. Family Charitable Fund supports their local Community Hospital Foundation, the Shock Trauma Air Rescue Service (STARS), the Alberta Cancer Foundation, the University of Alberta Hospital Foundation, the Canadian Wildlife Federation, the Heart and Stroke Foundation of Canada, the Canadian Liver Foundation, and their local public library.

Reflection:

What do you remember of your family's charitable habits while you were growing up?

_____

_____

_____

_____

_____

_____

_____

_____

_____

_____

_____

_____

_____

_____

_____

_____

_____

_____

_____

5

Donations and Taxes
for Individuals

*"In the symphony of life, charity is the
sweetest note." – Amelia Rodriguez*

IF YOU'RE READING THIS BOOK, YOU'VE PROBABLY made charitable donations before and have at least a passing familiarity with donation tax credits. However, a brief review may be in order.

First, let's clarify the difference between a tax deduction and a tax credit. A tax deduction reduces your taxable income; RRSP contributions are tax deductible. That means if you earned $100,000 in a year and made a $10,000 RRSP contribution, you get taxed as if you had only earned $90,000.

Tax deductions take place at your marginal tax bracket; that is the bracket where you were taxed on your last dollar of income. In the example above, the value of the RRSP contribution tax deduction is whatever the tax rate is for you, in your province, with an income between $90,000 and $100,000. Stated differently, the value of the deduction is the taxes that you didn't have to pay on that $10,000 of income.

Tax credits work differently and are generally assigned a fixed value by the federal and provincial governments, regardless of your income/tax bracket. The value of the credit is treated like a prepayment to your tax payable, so if you were already getting a refund on your tax return, you'll now get a larger one, and if you had tax payable then you'll owe less than before the credit was applied.

If you earn $100,000 and made a $10,000 charitable donation, you are still taxed on the full $100,000 of income, but then earn tax credits from the donation to reduce your total tax payable. It's important to note that tax credits do you no good if you wouldn't have owed any taxes in the first place. You can't make use of a credit against your taxes payable if there's nothing to pay!

When it comes to tax credits for charitable donations the federal government, as well as all the provinces and territories, give credits at one rate for the first $200 of donations in a tax year, and a higher rate for donations over $200. The notable exception is Alberta which just recently (in effect for the 2023 tax year) raised its credit on the first $200 donated from 10% to 60%. In a few cases (Federal, BC, and Quebec) there is also a third rate of credit set to equal the highest tax bracket for that jurisdiction, applicable to individuals with income in that top tax bracket – meaning that you're always getting at least a tax credit equal to your tax payable.

The Income Tax Act also restricts donations in a given tax year to 75% of your income for that year (there are special rules regarding giving at the time of death). Making a donation equal to 75% of your income would usually be more than enough (in combination with your other tax deductions and credits) to eliminate taxes payable for all but the very highest income Canadians.

This is a table of the donation tax credit rates in Canada for the 2024 tax year:

Tax Credit by Jurisdiction	First $200	>$200	>$200 with top bracket incomes
Federal	15.00%	29.00%	33.00%
AB	60.00%	21.00%	n/a
BC	5.06%	16.80%	20.50%
MB	10.80%	17.40%	n/a
NB	9.40%	17.95%	n/a
NL	8.70%	21.80%	n/a
NS	8.79%	21.00%	n/a
NT	5.90%	14.05%	n/a
NU	4.00%	11.50%	n/a
ON	5.05%	11.16%	n/a
PE	9.80%	16.70%	n/a
QC*	20.0%	24.00%	25.75%
SK	10.50%	14.50%	n/a
YT	6.40%	12.80%	n/a

*QC federal tax abatement reduction 16.5%

(Simplified because some jurisdictions have surtaxes. Most provinces use their lowest tax bracket as the rate for donations under $200 while others use an arbitrary rate. Things are more complex in Quebec. As with all financial and tax planning, get professional help with the details!)

Merging the federal and provincial/territorial credits, we get:

Jurisdiction	Combined donation tax credit rate		
	First $200	>$200	>$200 with top bracket incomes
AB	75.00%	50.00%	54.00%
BC	20.06%	45.80%	53.50%
MB	25.80%	46.40%	50.40%
NB	24.40%	46.95%	50.95%
NL	23.70%	50.80%	54.80%
NS	23.79%	50.00%	54.00%
NT	20.90%	43.05%	47.05%
NU	19.00%	40.50%	44.50%
ON	20.05%	40.16%	44.16%
PE	24.80%	45.70%	49.70%
QC*	35.00%	53.00%	58.75%
SK	25.50%	43.50%	47.50%
YT	21.40%	41.80%	45.80%

*QC federal tax abatement reduction 16.5%

There are a few ways we can leverage these tax rules to make our donating more efficient. First, donations are transferable between spouses. If you're filing taxes with a spouse, combine your donations on a single return in order to get more money over the $200 level. Again, Alberta has disrupted this long-standing piece of tax advice with their very high credit for donations under $200. If you're in Alberta, you'll want to make certain that each spouse is claiming at least $200 in donations (that is until the legislation potentially changes again!).

Second, if you're not in Alberta and you've had a year where your donations don't exceed $200, you can consider carrying them forward (you can carry donations forward up to five future tax years). In BC claiming $150 of donations in two consecutive years generates a credit each year of $30.09 each year. Claiming all $300 in the second year generates a credit of $85.92, a 42% increase over the $60.18 total from claiming over two years. That's 42% tax free profit!

The following table compares the tax credits for donations over $200 in a tax year with the marginal tax bracket for persons earning $75,000 and $200,000 per year:

Combined donation tax credit rates versus marginal tax rates for $75,000- and $200,000-income earners			
2023 rates by jurisdiction	>$200 donations combined rate	Marginal tax rate for $75,000	Marginal tax rate for $200,000
AB	50.00%	30.50%	42.32%
BC	45.80%	28.20%	46.12%
MB	46.40%	33.25%	46.72%
NB	46.95%	34.50%	48.82%
NL	50.80%	35.00%	47.12%
NS	50.00%	37.70%	50.32%
NT	43.05%	29.10%	43.37%
NU	40.50%	27.50%	40.42%
ON*	40.16%-46.41%	29.65%	48.29%
PE	45.70%	37.20%	47.69%
QC	53.00%	36.12%	50.23%
SK	43.50%	33.00%	43.82%
YT	41.80%	29.50%	42.25%

*Due to surtaxes in ON, for taxable incomes over $86,698 the effective tax credit is 13.39%, and 17.41% for incomes over $102,135 (rather than the 11.16% from the tax credits by jurisdiction table above) giving us the range shown here.

It's easy to see that in every case the donation credit rate for a person with $75,000 in taxable income is greater than their tax payable rate. At the $200,000 income level most jurisdictions are near break even, with the notable exceptions of Alberta where the credit is almost 8% greater than the marginal tax rate, and Ontario where it's 8% lower. Some jurisdictions have 10 or more tax brackets (because of slightly different bracket transitions between the provincial/territorial rate and the federal rate), so again, it's important to work through your personal details with a professional.

6

Purchasing a New Insurance Policy to Fund a Legacy Goal

"The truth of the matter is: you can create a great legacy, and inspire others, by giving to philanthropic organizations." – Michael Bloomberg

PERMANENT LIFE INSURANCE IS THE TYPE OF insurance that can stay in place on the covered person(s) for their entire life. That contrasts with term life insurance which usually is purchased in 10- or 20-year increments. Term insurance is very useful for covering obligations that have a fairly certain end to them (a mortgage for example). While term life insurance can usually be renewed at the end of that 10- or 20-year period, it's usually not renewable after your mid 60s and hence not an effective estate tax or philanthropic planning tool, as the normal Canadian life expectancy is 82-ish.

The two broad categories of permanent life insurance are whole life and universal life, which mostly vary by how the policies handle the "cash value" of the policy (term insurance does not have a cash value). Some Canadian insurance companies offer policies that are a hybrid of both types. In general, each company designs their products with a goal of including a unique set of features in order to make their offering stand out in the market. We're not going to dig deep into details here, it's more important just to introduce the ideas so that you can engage in a conversation with your financial and philanthropic advisor to customize a strategy for you.

It's also possible to develop a giving strategy based around using a life insurance policy you already have, and we'll tackle that topic in the chapter *Donating an Existing Insurance Policy*.

First, let's imagine a 30-year-old couple with large philanthropic goals, but not yet a large net worth. Using only $100 per month to purchase a universal life insurance policy from a major Canadian insurer, they can create a half million-dollar legacy. This policy is specifically designed to pay exactly $500,000 of death benefit that can be donated to charity, no matter when the last surviving member of the couple passes away.

As well, they only commit to 20 years of payments for the policy, even though the policy stays in place long past age 50 when they make their final premium payment. Twenty years of $100 per month equals just $24,000 of premiums paid to finance a $500,000 charitable donation!

Next, let's imagine starting at age 60 instead. This couple has higher cash flow that will persist into retirement based on decades of great financial planning; however, as they are 30 years older the life insurance policy will be correspondingly more expensive. For this couple, a policy that pays exactly $500,000 no matter when they've both passed away costs $500 per month, and again we've structured it to require premium payments for 20 years, though the policy stays in force forever. In this case $500 per month for 20 years totals

$120,000 of payments for a policy that will produce a $500,000 charitable donation.

In the chapter titled *Donate the policy death benefit or donate the policy and the premiums* we'll discuss the merits of donating the policy to charity, even before you pass away!

The examples I've used throughout this book are for non-smokers of average health, and when I give an example using a couple, I'm using a male-female couple. However, there are no barriers to single people or same sex couples employing these strategies.

People who smoke but are otherwise healthy can easily get insurance coverage but pay higher premiums due to the health effects of smoking. It is also possible for very healthy people to be offered lower insurance rates, and of course people suffering from serious health challenges will have trouble getting an application for life insurance approved. On the scale from average health to very poor health (so poor that an insurance company would not offer coverage) is a middle range where coverage may be offered at increased rates, so often coverage is still possible with worse than average health.

Don't assume that you cannot use an insurance-based strategy until you've made an insurance application and completed the medical underwriting process. Just because you don't feel as healthy at 60 as you did at 30 doesn't mean your health is poor compared to your average 60-year-old peer!

Why Do People Give?

*"Altruism is the heart's way of expressing
love for humanity." – Unknown*

IN 2014 THE CANADIAN ASSOCIATION OF GIFT Planners (CAGP)
published a report titled *The Philanthropic Conversation: Understanding Financial Advisors' Approaches and High Net Worth Individuals' Perspectives,* which listed the following motivations for giving
reported by a random sample of 178 high net worth donors:

- 55% Impact on community/world
- 50% Desire to give back
- 32% Passionate about a cause
- 23% Consider it an obligation of wealth
- 21% Reduce taxes
- 21% Religious or spiritual motivations
- 14% Asked by someone
- 11% Encourage children/future generations

In 2018 the Rideau Hall Foundation and Imagine Canada published their report *30 Years of Giving in Canada - The Giving Behaviour of Canadians: Who gives, how, and why?* which found similar responses when asking people why they donated. This report drew heavily upon Statistics Canada's General Social Survey program, with these results being reported in 2013 from a broad sample of Canadians of all ages, coast to coast:

- 91% Compassion towards those in need
- 88% Personal belief in the cause
- 82% Contribution to the community
- 67% Personally affected
- 45% Asked by someone
- 29% Religious obligations
- 26% Tax credit

As a financial advisor, I integrate tax planning into all the work my team does on behalf of the Canadians we serve. Still, it is heart warming to see that tax refunds are nowhere close to the top of either list of motivations for giving. We can use the tax laws to make our giving more effective or to help preserve our wealth for the benefit of other beneficiaries, but our financial planning decisions should be driven by our personal goals and values, not (just) our general dislike of paying taxes.

Throughout this book you will hear from real people like you about what motivated them to give, and you'll find no mention of tax reduction being the primary goal. Instead, you'll find reasons centered around love, legacy, and lifelong giving.

8

GIVING IN REAL LIFE

When Your Family is Four Legged: The Purple Cat Charitable Fund

"Let us try to teach generosity and altruism, because we are born selfish." – Richard Dawkins

ROXANNE IS A CLIENT WHO HAS WORKED with Simonson Team Private Wealth Management for more that two decades and was originally introduced by another client, someone with whom she was a co-worker at the time. One could make the case that your author's journey down the path to being a philanthropist began along with Roxanne in 2002 when they both participated in the Joints-In-Motion fundraiser for the Arthritis Society, during which they raised over $12,000 together and ran the Dublin Marathon in honour of someone afflicted by arthritis who was unable to run themselves.

Roxanne has persevered through many instances of bad luck during her life, coming to be a successful real estate and mortgage lending professional and owning a large tract of land overlooking the

North Saskatchewan River west of Edmonton. Roxanne shares her home with two dogs, three cats, and shares her land with numerous wildlife species, including many deer and a family of black bears.

While Roxanne's mother is still with her, her father has passed, and her sister died tragically young. Roxanne never started her own family and had recently been considering her legacy, given she has no children to pass her wealth down to. In her words "the thought of it was a little depressing. What is the point of working more?".

We had started discussing philanthropy in 2023, and in 2024 Roxanne created her charitable fund under the name Purple Cat, which has been her personal trademark for some time now. Knowing that she could still leave a legacy in some way gave Roxanne "a renewed sense of purpose".

Roxanne started her Donor Advised Fund with an initial cash donation, and she has also named the fund as the beneficiary of her registered retirement accounts. This will more than offset the taxes her estate would be responsible for based on those accounts being taxable when she passes away.

Roxanne agreed to be interviewed for this book. Here are some snippets from that conversation:

What do you remember about the approach your family took to giving in your youth? *Mom tended to donate to protect endangered species. I got that from her for sure.*

How did you choose which causes to support? *Animals have always made me feel safe, and not alone. Similarly, I've recently witnessed a close friend's severely autistic son benefit greatly from a service dog.*

What kind of impact do you hope to achieve through your philanthropic efforts? *As a human being we have to take care and support everyone. I was fortunate to be born where I was. That doesn't make me better than someone born into poverty.*

What advice would you offer to others who are considering making substantial charitable donations? *Sit quietly and contemplate what you want your legacy to look like. Talk to people you know and trust.*

What do you hope to accomplish by telling your story publicly? *I hope to generate awareness and discussion. I want to encourage people to be less isolated from each other in order to start conversations.*

The Purple Cat Charitable Fund supports Veterinarians Without Borders, the Canadian Wildlife Fund, and the Against Malaria Foundation.

Reflection:

What organization did you first donate to? What was the last organization you donated to? What's next?

_____

_____

_____

_____

_____

_____

_____

_____

_____

_____

_____

_____

_____

_____

_____

_____

_____

9

When to Give: Now, Ongoing, or Later?

"Money is not the only commodity that is fun to give. We can give time, we can give our expertise, we can give our love, or simply give a smile. What does that cost?" – Steve Goodier

WHEN CONSIDERING IMPLEMENTING A PHILANTHROPIC STRATEGY, THE three most important considerations will usually be our means, our timeline, and our objectives. Often our means and our timeline are very intricately connected as when we're older we have greater financial resources but less time to act.

If one is not starting from a position of excess wealth, then the giving strategies will be constrained to either a strategy that involves giving on an ongoing basis, or one that works towards building up to a larger future donation.

If one has the financial means to donate now, that should only be done after a careful financial planning analysis has determined that it is exceedingly unlikely that the donor will need those assets for personal use in the future. Further, it is often at least partially the case that donating money to a cause will leave less money for other beneficiaries of our estate. Good financial planning can help alleviate some or all of that net estate reduction by planning the giving to take the maximum advantage possible of the tax laws that support charitable giving.

Throughout this book you'll read examples of giving strategies based on real world work we've done with clients. All three timelines for giving (now, ongoing, and later) have their place in philanthropic planning. One theme will become apparent though: if you have the means to give now, then please give now!

Whether your philanthropic goal is to support a humanitarian cause, medical research, or animal welfare, there is a need for your support today. A $100,000 donation to a Donor Advised Fund that will support a foodbank with a $5000/year gift is more valuable to humankind than a $200,000 donation in 15 years. People who are hungry now need food now, not the promise of twice as much food in 15 years.

If you're concerned that giving now will deplete your estate and conflict with your goal of leaving money to your descendants, then it's important to consult with a financial advisor who holds both the CERTIFIED FINANCIAL PLANNER® and the MFA-Philanthropy® designations to help you design a financial and estate plan that can accomplish both.

10

Donating Directly from Excess Cash Flow

"If you think of life as like a big pie, you can try to hold the whole pie and kill yourself trying to keep it, or you can slice it up and give some to the people around you, and you still have plenty left for yourself." – Jay Leno

WHAT IF YOU DON'T HAVE A LARGE amount of assets to donate, but you have strong cash flow?

Sometimes a high-income household finds themselves in a position of excess cash flow, which brings the opportunity to start a charitable giving habit. This may be after getting a raise or a promotion, or maybe after paying off a debt and freeing up some space in the monthly budget. Balancing current needs with long term savings goals and philanthropic goals is a core part of the values based financial planning that a great advisory team will do with their clients.

Some have referred to compound growth as one of the wonders of the world, so let's take a look at what we can accomplish with a little compound giving!

The chart on the next page shows the growth of a Donor Advised Fund for someone who was able to make an initial deposit of $10,000[8], and then donate $500/month after that for a total of 25 years. The fund's investments earn a 7% return, and at the end of each year 5% is disbursed to charities

After 25 years the fund has already disbursed over $125,000 in annual gifts to charities. Donations from the Donor Advised Fund holder to the DAF have totalled $160,000 (at an after-tax cost of approximately half that) and the balance of the fund is projected to exceed $215,000, even after already disbursing the $125,000. The $215,000 balance at the end of year 25 means that in year 26 the Donor Advised Fund will disburse $10,750 to the causes the DAF supports. Those disbursements continue to gradually increase annually, even without any more contributions after year 25.

---

8    $10,000 is often the minimum initial deposit to start a DAF. Note that if you don't have that first $10,000 initially, then you can simply start saving the $500/month into a separate account from which you'll be able to make the starting $10,000 donation in less than two years!

Year	Starting Balance	Annual Contributions	Investment Gain	Disbursed to charity	Ending Balance
1	$10,000	$6,000	$910	$500	$16,410
2	$16,410	$6,000	$1,359	$821	$22,948
3	$22,948	$6,000	$1,816	$1,147	$29,617
4	$29,617	$6,000	$2,283	$1,481	$36,420
5	$36,420	$6,000	$2,759	$1,821	$43,358
6	$43,358	$6,000	$3,245	$2,168	$50,435
7	$50,435	$6,000	$3,740	$2,522	$57,654
8	$57,654	$6,000	$4,246	$2,883	$65,017
9	$65,017	$6,000	$4,761	$3,251	$72,527
10	$72,527	$6,000	$5,287	$3,626	$80,188
11	$80,188	$6,000	$5,823	$4,009	$88,001
12	$88,001	$6,000	$6,370	$4,400	$95,971
13	$95,971	$6,000	$6,928	$4,799	$104,101
14	$104,101	$6,000	$7,497	$5,205	$112,393
15	$112,393	$6,000	$8,078	$5,620	$120,851
16	$120,851	$6,000	$8,670	$6,043	$129,478
17	$129,478	$6,000	$9,273	$6,474	$138,277
18	$138,277	$6,000	$9,889	$6,914	$147,253
19	$147,253	$6,000	$10,518	$7,363	$156,408
20	$156,408	$6,000	$11,159	$7,820	$165,746
21	$165,746	$6,000	$11,812	$8,287	$175,271
22	$175,271	$6,000	$12,479	$8,764	$184,986
23	$184,986	$6,000	$13,159	$9,249	$194,896
24	$194,896	$6,000	$13,853	$9,745	$205,004
25	$205,004	$6,000	$14,560	$10,250	$215,314

11

Donations of Publicly Traded Securities

"If you're in the luckiest one percent of humanity, you owe it to the rest of humanity to think about the other 99 percent." – Warren Buffet

THERE'S ANOTHER POWERFUL SECTION OF INCOME TAX ACT that we can leverage when donating; donations of publicly traded securities may be entitled to an inclusion rate of zero on any capital gain resulting from donation. That means we won't have to pay any tax on the profit we earned if the price of the investment increased during the period we held it. Such securities are most often stocks or investment funds, however the full list from CRA's website is:

- a share of the capital stock of a mutual fund corporation,
- a unit of a mutual fund trust,
- an interest in a related segregated fund trust,
- a prescribed debt obligation that is not a linked note,

- a share, debt obligation, or right listed on a designated stock exchange.

Typically, when we sell an investment that is not in a tax shelter (RRSPs, RRIFs, RESPs, and TFSAs are tax shelters) we are required to include 50% (or sometimes more based on changes introduced in the 2024 Federal Budget) of the profit from the sale in our taxable income for that tax year. For example, a stock purchase of $1000 followed some time later by a sale for $3000 results in $2000 of profit, and $1000 of that is reported as income on our tax return for the year of sale. However, if we donated those stocks directly to charity, the income inclusion rate is set to 0% instead of 50% (and the other $1000 of profit is tax-free).

Example: in Alberta at the 30.5% tax bracket, if you sold that stock yourself, you'd owe an extra $305 in taxes from the $1000 included in income. Then, if you donated the remaining $2695 to charity (and already had over $200 donated that year) you'd get a donation credit for 50% of that, or $1347.50, and net a tax reduction of $1042.50 (after you pay the $305 tax on the capital gain). Net result: $2650 to charity at a cost to you of $1957.50 (the $3000 value of your stock less $1042.50 of net tax credits). See the chart below.

If you instead donated the stock directly to charity (and remember if you have a Donor Advised Fund, it is administered by a Parent Foundation, which itself is a charity) then all $3000 goes to charity and you earn a donation credit of $1500, while none of the capital gain from the stock is included in your income so you have no more taxes payable. In this case, your cost to donate $3000 to charity is only $1500 after the donation credit. The charitable cause you care about benefits more and it costs you less!

Alberta 30.5% tax bracket	Sell, then donate the cash proceeds	Donate the shares directly to the charity
Purchase price	$1000	$1000
Sale price	$3000	$3000
Profit	$2000	$2000
Taxable gain	$1000	$0
Taxes payable	-$305	$0
Net to charity	**$2695**	**$3000**
Tax credit 50%	$1347.50	$1500
Your after-tax cost	**$1957.50**	**$1500**

Stock options, especially employee stock options, are a very special case that require careful handling. If you're interested in donating stock options that are "in the money," please consult with a qualified financial advisor and an experienced tax preparer to ensure the correct process is followed in order to minimize tax payable and maximize the donation.

12

Child Free Estate Planning:
The Camrenlee Memorial Fund

"The seeds of love and charity blossom into gardens of joy." – Benjamin Hayes

IF YOU WERE A CLIENT OF MINE between 1999 and 2016, chances are good that you'll remember my assistant, Cathy. Cathy lost her father when she was in high school and grew up very close to her mother whom I had the pleasure of meeting several times before she passed. Once Cathy retired, our client-advisor conversations started down a path discussing what she wanted to do with her assets after she passed away.

Cathy liked the idea of leaving a philanthropic legacy in the name of her family. With some additional financial planning work, we were able to show her that she could set up a Donor Advised Fund now, without threatening her financial security throughout retirement. She was able to start the fund with an initial gift, and then we set her DAF as the beneficiary of some of the higher taxed assets (specifically the registered retirement accounts) that will be in her estate. By donating any remaining amounts in these accounts upon her passing, she will be able to offset the taxes that would otherwise be payable by her estate.

Cathy had inherited some Canadian stocks from her mother. By donating the stocks directly to the Parent Foundation as her initial contribution, she was able to avoid paying capital gains tax on the appreciated value of those investments, as well as getting tax credits equal to 50% of the donation. In this way Cathy was able to make the initial $10,000 donation to her Donor Advised Fund at an out-of-pocket cost of less than half that amount.

Cathy named her DAF the Camrenlee Memorial Fund by taking letters from her and her parent's names. She especially liked that she could choose her Beneficiary Charities now and retain the option to update them in the future.

Cathy agreed to be interviewed for this book because she appreciated the work I did as her financial advisor in bringing this idea to her, and she wants more people to learn about philanthropic planning. Here are some snippets from that conversation:

What do you remember about the approach your family took to giving in your youth? *Mom always gave to charity, particularly Hope Mission. She had a thing about people not going hungry.*

What influenced your decision to make substantial charitable donations? *I don't have children to pass my estate along to, so it is nice to know that the money will go to causes I care about, supporting the community I live in.*

What causes did you choose, and why? *The Food Bank to support the community and honour my mother. Cancer research because I'm a breast cancer survivor. The War Amps because I feel this is a lower profile organization needs support too.*

Have your motivations or perspectives changed over the years? *When you get older more things come to mind, plus you have more resources.*

In your opinion, what role should individuals play in addressing societal issues through philanthropy? *I think I have a good life. I think it's important for people to give back. How much money do you really have to have? We should help people who are less fortunate than we are.*

The Camrenlee Memorial Fund supports the Alberta Cancer Foundation, the Edmonton Food Bank, the Salvation Army of Alberta, and the War Amputations of Canada.

Reflection:

Do you tend to make your charitable activities visible to friends and family, or do you prefer to keep them quiet? Why? What would happen if you made them more public than they are now?

_____

_____

_____

_____

_____

_____

_____

_____

_____

_____

_____

_____

_____

_____

_____

_____

_____

_____

13

The Government's Role in the Charitable Sector

"Darkness cannot drive out darkness: Only light can do that. Hate cannot drive out hate: Only love can do that." – Martin Luther King Jr.

Regulator

NO ONE SHOULD BE SURPRISED TO HEAR that one of the important roles government plays in the charitable sector is regulation. This includes both the tax laws around how charities operate and the donation credits we've discuss in other chapters, and also the very rules that define what a charity is or is not.

Charities must use their resources for charitable activities and have a charitable purpose that falls into one or more of the following categories:

- The relief of poverty,
- The advancement of education,

- The advancement of religion; or
- Other purposes that benefit the community.

That last category is rather broad and encompasses all the health care and medical research charities, for example.

The federal government maintains a webpage full of useful information on charities, even including instructions to help with starting a charitable organization; a search for 'CRA services charity' online should get you right there. That page also links to a list of charities that are in good standing with CRA, and therefore eligible to issue donation receipts. It is always a good idea to confirm that a charity you wish to support directly or through a Donor Advised Fund is on the approved list.

Donor

Many Canadians would probably be surprised to learn that government is by far the largest funder of charities in Canada. According to *The Giving Report (2018)* published by CandaHelps.org, charities in Canada received operating funds from:

- 68% Government funding (90% of this is from provincial governments),
- 9% Fundraising via sales of goods & services,
- 6% Receipted gifts – donations made by individuals and corporations entitled to a receipt,
- 3% Non-receipted gifts & fundraising / international gifts – donations through a means that do not generate a tax receipt and gifts from outside of Canada,
- 2% Inter-charity revenue – common examples of charities that help fund other charities include public and private foundations and the United Way, and

- 12% Other (might include investment income or revenue from the sale of assets).

Note that the 'Inter-charity revenue' line includes gifts from foundations, and that's where a Donor Advised Fund would fit in.

At a glance, this list might almost be discouraging because it looks like the impact of individual giving is insignificant next to government funding. However, a deeper dive into the numbers contained in *The Giving Report* shows that the very largest charities (those having over 200 employees) total only 1% of charities, yet they receive 85% of all government funding. Large health and education focussed charities are frequently the organizations that receive the most government support; over 87% of all government funding to charity goes to those two sectors.

Health and education are important causes; however, the very smallest charities (10 employees or less) are left to depend on volunteer hours and public donations. These smallest charities receive, on average, 33% of their revenue from direct donations. In the chapter *Donate via Lump Sums or DAF Distributions* we will discuss how organizations need ongoing cash flow from donors to support their operations, with food banks and animal shelters being great examples of charities that depend heavily on volunteers (to reduce funds spent on staffing) and have consistent cash flow needs to support ongoing operations.

One might ask, since governments are the largest funders of charities, why don't we just pay more in taxes and the government could use that revenue to give more to the charities? Or for that matter, why doesn't the government just use tax revenue to provide the programs themselves instead of leaving it to charities? The answer to those public policy type questions could fill another book, and those topics are sensitive and potentially divisive, depending on your personal values.

Your author can only offer a simple question: would you rather a system where the government taxed us more to finance a broader range of programs, inserting an expensive level of bureaucracy in between you and the end charities, to fund causes that may not match the priorities of you and your family? Or would you rather the current system, one that allows you to directly support the causes you choose, while benefitting from generous tax credits? I think the answer is clear.

14

Death and Taxes

*"Remember that the happiest people are
not those getting more, but those giving
more." – H. Jackson Brown Jr.*

IN CANADA THERE IS NO TAX THAT is defined in legislation as an "Estate Tax," but functionally we must consider two government related expenses when we pass away: our final income tax bills and probate costs.

Income tax

When we pass away, we are deemed to have "disposed" of all our assets at the moment of death. Tax professionals refer to this as a deemed disposition; even though your assets haven't been sold, you're going to be taxed as if they were. RRSPs and RRIFs are deemed to have been withdrawn, properties sold, investments sold, and if you're a small business owner, your shares in your business are deemed to be sold too. There are many opportunities to roll over property to a surviving spouse without the taxable disposition, so upon the first death of in a couple there is usually little or no taxes payable.

Assets that do not pass to a spouse or directly to a joint owner (for assets held in joint tenancy) transfer from the deceased individual to their estate. Estates are a form of trust (a testamentary trust), and each calendar year your estate exists it will be required to file a tax return and remit any taxes payable.

It's really upon the death of someone without a surviving spouse where the taxes may land hard. In this book when we talk about estate taxes or taxes at death, we'll be referring to both the taxes payable on the person's final tax return (aptly referred to in legislation as the terminal return), as well as taxes paid by their estate between the death of the taxpayer and the final distribution of assets out of the estate, to the beneficiaries.

Many excellent reference pieces are available to assist Canadians with estate planning. We suggest that your best tool is a competent financial planning team who can assist you in estimating your estate taxes, providing both an estimate for if you were to die unexpectedly today, and one based on your statistical life expectancy.

Probate Fees

Probate fees are simply the cost of having a will validated at your provincial courthouse. A probated will gives authority to the executor to begin the process of settling the estate, including dealing with financial institutions and Canada Revenue Agency.

Probating the will is an essential step for all but the smallest estates; often financial institutions will not require a probated will to settle very small account balances.

Probate fees are a matter of provincial legislation and vary greatly from province to province. Several provinces charge a fixed or a sliding fee that one might consider a "reasonable" amount, while other provinces assess based on a percentage of the estate, drifting more towards a tax than a fee:

- Alberta* (sliding fee):
  - Minimum $35 for an estate of $10,000 or less.
  - Maximum $525 for an estate over $250,000.

- British Columbia (fee plus percentage):
  - Nothing for estates of $25,000 or less.
  - Over $25,000 there is a $200 filing fee, plus:
    » 0.6% of value from $25,000 to $50,000.
    » 1.4% of value over $50,000.
  - No maximum.

- Manitoba eliminated probate fees for applications made after November 6th, 2020.

- Ontario (percentage):
  - Nothing for estates of $50,000 or less.
  - 1.5% on amounts over $50,000.
  - No maximum.

- PEI* (sliding fee up to $100,000, then add percentage):
  - Minimum $50 for an estate of $10,000 or less.
  - $400 for an estate of $50,000 to $100,000.
  - Plus 0.4% on amounts over $100,000.
  - No maximum.

- New Brunswick* (sliding fee up to $20,000, then add percentage):
  - Minimum $25 for an estate valued $5000 or less.
  - $100 for an estate of $15,000 to $20,000.
  - 0.5% on amounts over $20,000.
  - No maximum.

- Newfoundland and Labrador (percentage):
  - 0.6% (minimum $60).
  - No maximum.

- Nunavut* (sliding fee):
  - Minimum $30 for an estate of $10,000 or less.
  - Maximum $435 for an estate over $250,000.

- NWT* (sliding fee):
  - Minimum $30 for an estate of $10,000 or less.
  - Maximum $435 for an estate over $250,000.

- Nova Scotia* (sliding fee up to $100,000, then add percentage):
  - Minimum $85.60 for an estate valued $10,000 or less.
  - $1002.65 for an estate of $50,000 to $100,000.
  - 1.695% on amounts over $100,000.
  - No maximum.

- Quebec does not charge probate fees, but there are court filing fees to be paid. The 2024 fee is $223.

- Saskatchewan (flat fee plus percentage):
  - $25 filing fee.
  - 0.7% of estate value.
  - No maximum.

- Yukon (flat fee):
  - A fee may or may not be charged for an estate worth less than $25,000.
  - $140 flat fee for an estate value over $25,000.

*For brevity, in provinces with a sliding fee only the highest and lowest tiers are listed here. Data sourced from the respective government websites.

It is worth noting that in BC, Newfoundland and Labrador, and PEI that the probate fee is based on the gross value of your estate – that is to say the sum of your assets, regardless of any debts. In the rest of the country outstanding mortgages are deducted from the amount subject to the fee calculation.

From an estate planning point of view, it's easy to see the dichotomy in Canada. Clients and their financial planners in Manitoba, Alberta, Quebec, and all three Territories need not worry about planning to minimize probate fees. In all the other provinces, especially BC, Nova Scotia, and Ontario, estimating probate fee costs and having a plan to both minimize them and pay them when the time comes is an important part of the estate planning process.

Philanthropic planning can play an important role in reducing both estate taxes and probate costs. In the next two chapters I'll share how we've helped clients do just that.

15

Death and Taxes: When You Know They Are Going to Arrive at the Same Time

"In the garden of humanity, charity is the sweetest fruit." – Abigail Coleman

IN THE UPCOMING CHAPTER TITLED GIVING IN *Real Life - Give now or later? The Frank Family Fund,* I will describe a situation where it does not make sense for the clients to wait to donate via their final estate settlement as directed by their wills, because there is projected to be little or no tax payable in their estate.

Sometimes though, we have a great deal of certainty regarding the taxes that will be due upon our death, and a life insurance-based donation strategy can be of great value to offset those taxes. A relatively common example of this is a family cabin. Unlike a primary residence which is exempt from taxes upon being sold, a second piece of property is taxed similarly to a conventional financial investment.

Here's a simplified example loosely based upon several cases I've seen in my career:

- Mom and Dad purchased a lake lot for $20,000 in the 1980s,
- They spent $125,000 building a cottage on the lot shortly after,
- In the 1990s they added a garage for $50,000,
- Over the years they spent another $5000 on capital improvements for which they have documentation.

The sum of that spending is $200,000, and that's what we call the Adjusted Cost Base (ACB) of the property. Twenty years later when we sat down with Mom and Dad to review their estate plan, the cabin had long been an integral part of the family's life. It is a place where their children spent (and now their grandchildren spend) summers making countless fond memories of "going to the lake".

While preparing the estate projection, our team noted that the current market value of the cabin was now $800,000. Projecting forward another 20 years to Mom's actuarial life expectancy, they estimated a value at her death of $1,200,000. Assuming Mom lived longer (as odds are that women live longer than men) her estate would realize a $1,000,000 capital gain on the cabin, of which $500,000 (50%) would be reported as income on her final tax return.

Our tax preparer estimated that this gain on Mom's final return would lead to $225,000 in tax payable on the deemed disposition of the cabin at her death. We also noted that Mom's will says the title of the cabin passes to the children according to her wishes, and that there was no plan to sell the cabin because the children (and grandchildren!) want to continue to enjoy it.

This situation begs an obvious question? Who was going to pay the $225,000 of taxes, and where was the cash going to come from if the cabin wasn't actually sold? Our cash flow projections estimated that at the end of Mom's life, that Mom and Dad's assets would have been depleted by normal retirement spending, including extra costs for care near the end of their lives. At first glance it looked like the kids would be forced into a position to either borrow money or be required to dip into their own retirement savings to pay the taxes.

This is a situation where a good financial planning team will bring forward permanent life insurance as a strategy for the clients to consider. A life insurance policy that pays out after both parents have passed away can provide the money to pay the taxes for pennies on the dollar. Here's an example:

- A permanent insurance policy paying $150,000 costs $6200/yr.
- $150,000 approximately equals the tax bill on the cabin if Mom and Dad were killed in a vehicle accident tomorrow.
- The investment component of the policy increases the total value of the policy over time. In 25 years, right around Mom's normal life expectancy, the policy is projected to pay out $225,000. This matches the projected tax bill.
- In this case, we effectively hire the insurance company to pay the taxes, allowing the cabin to transfer smoothly to the kids.

There was more to the estate planning conversation though: Mom and Dad had also expressed interest in creating a family legacy fund. Both lost parents to cancer and they felt strongly about donating to fund cancer curing research.

This led the planning team to present another option: double the size of the insurance policy and donate the proceeds to a Donor Advised Fund. The tax credit from the donation would offset the taxes payable by Mom's projected estate, and the legacy DAF would then be administered by the children, and eventually the grandchildren, etc.

Here is a comparison of the three scenarios.

Strategy:	No Plan: Borrow to pay taxes, pay off over 15 years at 5%	Basic Plan: Buy insurance to cover taxes, pay for 15 years	Advanced Plan: Buy insurance to create the family legacy DAF, pay for 15 years.
Cost to family before death (i.e., insurance premiums)		$6200/yr. x 15 years =$93,000	$12,000/yr. x 15 years = $180,000
Cost to family after death	$1800/m x 12m x 15 years =$270,000	$0	$0
Taxes payable at death	$225,000	$225,000	$0
Money donated to family legacy DAF	$0	$0	$450,000
Donation tax credit	$0	$0	$225,000
Annual disbursement to charity	$0	$0	$22,500

Results:

No Plan: Doing nothing and leaving the kids to borrow money to cover the estate taxes costs the family $270,000, based on the payment required on a 15-year mortgage on the cabin to cover the taxes due.

Basic Plan: Taking out insurance to cover the tax bill costs the family $93,000, demonstrating the amazing power of insurance to prepay the tax bill for **35 cents on the dollar**. However, the legacy goal for cancer research is unfulfilled in this scenario.

Advanced Plan: If we use insurance to make the donation to the Legacy Fund, then the taxes can be completely offset, and the Donor Advised Fund will start by disbursing $22,500 per year to charities (contrast that to $21,600 per year in loan payments in the first scenario). The cost to the family for this is estimated at $180,000, still less than what the original tax bill is forecast to be!

Stated another way, the family can save $90,000 out of pocket compared to the No Plan scenario, while creating $450,000 of good in the world. Even though my team and I have done this work for years, it is still jaw dropping to work through a case and see how powerful these strategies are in real life.

Note: In June 2024 the capital gains inclusion rate for gains over $250,000 was increased from 50% to 66.67%. If that legislation survives future changes in government, then the tax risk to the family cabin is even greater.

16

Give Now or Later?
The Frank Family Fund

"True happiness comes from having a sense of inner peace and contentment, which in turn must be achieved by cultivating altruism, love and compassion, and by eliminating anger, selfishness and greed." – Dalai Lama

DONORS OFTEN WRESTLE WITH THE QUESTION OF is it better to give now, or later? As financial advisors, my team's first priority is to ensure that the clients we serve have the financial means to live out their lives with dignity and independence. Once we're certain that donating now won't create a cashflow shortfall later in life, we can open a discussion regarding gifting plans. If there is a risk of creating a cashflow shortfall, then we can pivot to discussing a gift via an estate designation and hold the capital in reserve for as long as they are alive.

Once you've determined, with the aid of your financial planning team, that you have adequate cash flow coverage for retirement (including a generous margin of error over a generous life expectancy) then you can have a conversation about a planned giving strategy. After our analysis we often find that our clients can have more impact with small donations now, than they can later with a large lump sum donation via the estate.

Mr. and Mrs. Frank are a lovely couple whose family I have worked with for over two decades and four generations. We recently reviewed their will[9], and noted a clause stating that 10% of their estate was to be split between eight charities which were listed in the will.

The first problem was that the will was a few years old, and upon review Mr. and Mrs. Frank noted that there were at least two charities that they would not choose to support today. The second problem was that, while recognizing that tax advantages are not the primary motivation for giving for many Canadians, Mr. and Mrs. Frank's estate was unlikely to have any significant amount of tax payable, causing the charitable tax credit for donating to be wasted.

We proposed to Mr. and Mrs. Frank that they set up a family legacy fund immediately. This would accomplish several goals:

- The charities they cared about would start receiving money now, not in 27 years, which was their combined projected life expectancy,
- In the future if they decide to change the charitable organizations they wish to support, they only need file a update form for their Donor Advised Fund (saving legal fees that would be incurred when modifying a will), and

---

9   Good financial advisors get copies of their clients' wills because your will is your final and perhaps most important financial planning document. Most people consider it as a legal document, and it is in the literal sense, but what's the point of that legal document? To make a final distribution of your personal wealth; so, it is certainly a financial planning document as well.

- They can involve their children, and especially their grandchildren, in the giving process while they are still alive!

To help Mr. and Mrs. Frank decide, we projected a comparison of the 'as is' scenario, versus our recommendation. In the 'as is' case, we projected Mr. and Mrs. Frank to have a net estate of $1,400,000, which meant their executor would direct one tenth, $140,000, to be split between the list of charities in the will (which may or may not reflect the charities that Mr. and Mrs. Frank wanted to support at that time). Their four children would then split the remaining $1,260,000 ($315,000 each). The $140,000 donation would create a $70,000 tax credit, but without any tax payable in the estate, the tax credit would likely be wasted.

Mr. and Mrs. Frank have registered retirement assets that are not essential to their retirement cash flow because of the stability of income they are lucky to enjoy from a workplace pension and their combined CPP and OAS pensions. However, those retirement accounts come with forced minimum annual withdrawals, creating taxes payable every year. It was our recommendation that Mr. and Mrs. Frank take $10,000 of this cash flow each year for the next 27 years and donate that to a family legacy fund, set up via a Donor Advised Fund.

In the proposed case, Mr. and Mrs. Frank donate $10,000 annually and can utilize a tax credit of $5000 each year. Over the 27 years of projected life expectancy $270,000 is donated, and $135,000 of tax credits are utilized. The after-tax cost of donation nets out to $135,000, which is slightly less than the $140,000 that would have been donated via their wills as they are currently written. Donating sooner rather than later has two other notable effects beyond the substantial tax benefit. First, charities that Mr. and Mrs. Frank care about start receiving support sooner rather than later. Second, some of the investment growth that would have occurred in Mr. and Mrs. Frank's personal name now occurs in the family legacy fund, reducing taxes payable while Mr. and Mrs. Frank are alive.

Their final estate in the proposed case is reduced from $1,260,000 after donations to $950,000, a decrease of $310,000. Each of the four children still receives an estimated $237,500, which is $77,500 less each than in the current scenario. It's worth noting that by the time we estimate both parents will have passed, the four children will range in age from 60 to 70 years old. Likely by that point in life the children will be financially stable, and not depending on an inheritance to fund their own retirement.

While there is a decrease in the estate of $310,000 this is offset by some benefits. By the time we estimate they both will have passed away, they will already have donated $270,000 to the family legacy fund. With a 5% disbursement rate this means $218,000 will have been donated over the years **before** Mr. and Mrs. Frank pass away. That compares quite favourably to the $140,000 estate donation in the 'as is' case, which would not benefit the causes Mr. and Mrs. Frank care about for over two and a half decades to come. Not only that, but the family legacy fund balance upon the final death is also estimated to be $340,000! The year after Mr. and Mrs. Frank have both passed, the legacy fund will distribute another $17,000, an amount which will continue and gradually increase, forever!

Combining the pre-death donations and the value of the legacy upon death, Mr. and Mrs. Frank can do over $450,000 of good in the world while reducing the inheritance of each child by $77,500. Additionally, Mr. and Mrs. Frank will have created a legacy of giving that will last for generations to come. Grandchildren, great-grandchildren, and generations to come will learn the value of giving from Mr. and Mrs. Frank, even if they never get to meet their great (or great-great) grandparents!

Give now or later? If you have the means, now is almost always better.

Reflection:

*What past events impacted you and your family
in a way that affects how you give now?*

_____

_____

_____

_____

_____

_____

_____

_____

_____

_____

_____

_____

_____

_____

_____

_____

_____

_____

_____

_____

_____

17

I've Got My Own DAF, Now What?

"The true meaning of life is to plant trees, under whose shade you do not expect to sit." – Nelson Henderson

Once your Donor Advised Fund is up and running you can elect to do nothing and watch it grow, or over time you can decide to modify.

If you do nothing, then your DAF carries on indefinitely according to the instructions you gave when you set it up. The investment fund in the DAF account will remain in the originally designated investment fund, it will pay out at the designated time of year, at the designated rate, to the designated charity or charities.

If you pass away without a joint account holder, or a designated successor, the above scenario is what will happen to your DAF. In the event that one of your Beneficiary Charities ceases to exist or perhaps merges with another organization, the board of directors of the Parent Foundation will select a replacement charity that aligns with the purpose of the original charity.

It's likely that most Donor Advised Funds will have a successor account holder, however we can imagine some scenarios where the original donor may not need or want a successor. Perhaps the donor wants to support one of those causes we identified that needs ongoing funding (a food bank or an animal shelter for example). Perhaps a donation is being made in the memory of a loved one who died from a rare disease, and the donor wants to support ongoing research in that field for as long as it takes to find a cure.

Most often the original donor intends for the fund to continue for an indefinite period and wants only to reserve the right to adjust the DAF if something changes. Any of the items from the original paperwork can be changed, including even the account holders themselves – they can turn over control of the DAF while they are still alive if they choose. They can adjust the Beneficiary Charities, replacing ones that have fallen out of favour, adapt the BC list to new personal priorities, or add more BCs as the DAF grows in value. When new investment options are presented, they can decide to make changes or leave the account as it is.

My favourite version of the Donor Advised Fund is the family legacy fund. Perhaps a set of grandparents start a DAF with an initial donation of $200,000. At a 5% disbursement rate, that starts generating $10,000 a year for gifting to the Beneficiary Charities, and that amount will likely gradually increase over time. Grandma and Grandpa want to both focus on supporting some BCs that are important to them, and also teach their grandchildren about the importance of giving back. What they decide to do is direct half the disbursements themselves and break the remaining $5000 into five shares that they are willing to adjust each year, based on input from the family.

Imagine the conversation at the Thanksgiving Day dinner table when Grandma and Grandpa ask the family what they are thankful for, and then ask the children and grandchildren to think of others less fortunate than themselves. Next, they invite everyone to nominate charities they think are worthy of support and allocate the five $1000 shares to those causes. The following year the grandchildren will know to come prepared with proposals, which leads them to be more aware of both the need in the world, and the good fortune they've enjoyed being part of such a wonderful family. That is priceless!

18
GIVING IN REAL LIFE

Generational Giving in Action: The COLIEMYN Fund

"No matter what happens in life, be good to people. Being good to people is a wonderful legacy to leave behind." – Taylor Swift

BRUCE AND NICOLETTE ARE MORE RECENT CLIENTS of Simonson Team Private Wealth Management, having been referred to us by a friend who at that time had been a client for more than two decades. They are the parents of two darling young girls. With good jobs and strong saving habits, Bruce and Nicolette were already on the path to financial freedom when Nicolette's last surviving parent passed, and she inherited the remains of her parents' wealth.

The death of a loved one is always difficult, and this situation was accompanied by extra layers of emotion. Nicolette's parents were hard working Dutch immigrants who were more likely to save extra money than to spend it on "fun" things like vacations. After her father's passing, she wondered how to use this money to honour the memory of her parents.

I proposed a memorial fund to Bruce and Nicolette as a means of keeping those memories alive and including the next generation in the process. While young, their daughters were certainly old enough to understand the concept of giving back and perceptive enough that they had already seen ways in which giving back has had a positive impact on the world.

This may well be my favourite real-life example of a classic family legacy fund: the parents created the Donor Advised Fund using money inherited from the grandparents, and the grandchildren chose the charities. The girls will also take over guidance of the fund in the future. Every year or two when the family reviews the Beneficiary Charities they've chosen, they'll be reminded that the source of this beneficence was their grandparents' hard work.

Nicolette is one of several siblings, and the family had long used the word COLIEMYN to refer to themselves. Using the first two letters of each parent's name, and the first letter of each child's name created a word that was pronounceable in Dutch. This was the name of the family boat, it was printed on coffee mugs around the house, and Nicolette even paid to name a star COLIEMYN on her parent's 45th wedding anniversary. This fund is another way the family's legacy of love will carry on forever.

Bruce and Nicolette agreed to be interviewed for this book. Here are some snippets from that conversation:

What do you remember about your family's approach to giving in your youth? **Bruce:** *More volunteering than giving, particularly working bingos for charities. And of course, supporting the UNICEF campaign every Halloween.*

How have your motivations regarding charitable giving changed over the years? **Bruce:** *We first encountered this idea when we learned* *our friends (the ones who referred us to you) had created a fund like this years ago. Before that we just gave "normally," a little here, a little there, without a thoughtful strategy.*

What inspired you to become more active philanthropically and make the significant donation now? **Nic:** *Your suggestion to create a legacy fund that the girls will carry on really fit our value set, especially getting them involved in choosing the charities now and over time.* **Bruce:** *I like that we can now screen random donation requests by saying that we only give through our private foundation *laughs*.* **Nic:** *I think about how cheap my parents were through their whole lives. They wanted to make sure the family was taken care of first. I think now that some is left over, they'd be okay with donating a portion.*

What causes did you choose to support, and how did you select them? **Nic:** *The girls can relate to animals, and we want them to be aware that not every kid is as lucky as they are with respect to having a good home, good health, and good finances.*

What role do you feel individuals have to play in addressing societal issues through philanthropy? **Nic:** *Taylor Swift donates in every city she has a concert in. People with lots of money can make an impact by giving back.* **Bruce:** *People who work at non-profits find the work rewarding because it's good work. Similarly, it feels good to donate to good causes.* **Nic:** *People like us who have the means to give should do so. Rich corporations should give more.*

What advice would you offer to others who are considering making substantial charitable donations? **Bruce:** *Do it! It's not complex or difficult, just do it.* **Nic:** *Be comfortable with the amount. You can always start small and donate more later. Just get started.*

What do you hope to accomplish by telling your story publicly? **Nic:** *More people should know about this. We would not have come up with the idea ourselves. It's good that you give people time to think about it and that you make it as easy as possible.*

The **COLIEMYN Fund** supports the Edmonton Humane Society and the Make a Wish Foundation of Canada.

Reflection:

What kind of impact do you hope to make on the world with your charitable giving?

_____

_____

_____

_____

_____

_____

_____

_____

_____

_____

_____

_____

_____

_____

_____

_____

_____

_____

19

Donate the Policy Death Benefit, or Donate the Policy and the Premium Payments?

"I choose to rise up out of that storm and see that in moments of desperation, fear and helpless-ness, each of us can be a rainbow of hope, doing what we can to extend ourselves in kindness and grace to one another." – Oprah Winfrey

As discussed in other chapters, using insurance to donate is an effective way to do good, and there are multiple strategies that can be employed. This chapter deals with creating a new policy for a charitable giving plan. To learn about donating an existing policy that is being repurposed for charitable giving, please see the chapter *Donating an existing insurance policy.*

Many charities will accept the donation of an insurance policy if you commit to making donations equal to the premium payments. Remember how the 30-year-old couple from the chapter *Creating a new insurance policy to fund a legacy goal,* purchased an insurance policy with the intent of donating the death benefit? Instead, they could go through the insurance application process and once the policy is approved, transfer ownership of the policy to the charity. In that case they would commit to making a $100/m donation to the charity for the 20 years that premium payments are required, and the charity uses the $100 to pay the monthly insurance premium.

In this scenario, instead of the last surviving partner's estate receiving a $500,000 charitable donation credit, they receive a donation receipt from the charity each year for $1200. The result - a half a million dollars of donations - is the same, only the amount and timing of the donation tax credit changes.

While it is possible to find a charity that will accept the donation of an insurance policy, many charities may be hesitant to enter into an arrangement like this because of the risk that the donors do not complete the 20-year premium payment donation commitment. In the previous case of the 30-year-old couple and the $100 per month insurance premium for the $500,000 death benefit, if they had the means they could donate the entire $24,000 to the charity up front. That removes any risk to the charity with respect to being committed to 20 years' worth of $100 per month premiums. This approach may originate from a scenario where a person has received an inheritance and wants to leverage a modest amount such as $24,000 into a huge $500,000 donation in memory of the person they inherited from.

It is also possible to use an annuity to assure the premiums will be paid. An insurance annuity is a contract between you and an insurance company. Here's how it works in simple terms:

- You make a single lump sum payment (most common) or a series of payments to the insurance company (less common).

- In return, the insurance company promises to pay you a regular income. This income can start immediately or at some point in the future.
- The goal of an annuity is to provide a steady stream of income, typically during retirement, but in this case, we intend to use the income stream to pay the insurance premium for 20 years.
- The amount of income you receive can be fixed or variable, depending on the type of annuity you choose. In this example we would want to purchase an annuity that pays exactly $100 per month for 20 years.

At the time of writing, an annuity that would pay the $100 monthly life insurance premium payments could be purchased for less than $20,000. In this case the donor would first apply for the insurance and, after being approved, buy the annuity. Then the donor would donate both the life insurance and the annuity contract to the charity and receive a donation receipt for the amount paid for the annuity. Going this route could permit a future $500,000 memorial donation for the current cost of a $20,000 donation.

One interesting variation of the strategy is a special type of insurance policy designed exactly for this type of hypothetical case where the couple wants to use $24,000 in a single transaction to fund an insurance policy that will be used to make a sizable charitable donation. In this case, the policy is a form of conventional whole life insurance with a death benefit payout that starts low and increases over time.

The initial value of the policy is about $56,000 dollars, and increases over time as follows:

Policy year	Age of clients	Projected death benefit
Start	30	$56,000
10	40	$75,000
20	50	$103,000
30	60	$144,000
40	70	$202,000
50	80	$287,000
60	90	$412,000
70	100	$607,000

At the time of writing only one Canadian insurer has launched a product like this, however we will not be surprised if more follow suit.

Permanent life insurance is an amazingly versatile tool that knowledgeable financial advisory teams often suggest to clients for consideration when it comes to estate, tax, and charitable planning.

20

When it's Not About the Money: The M. Family Charitable Fund

"The heart that gives is never empty." – Alice Nelson

During my first year as a financial advisor, I stayed in the military as a member of the Army Reserve. I served with Richard, who by day taught at a university in Edmonton. Richard was well liked, as he was an intelligent, caring, and jovial leader.

In the mid-late 2010s Richard was diagnosed with Fronto-temporal Degeneration (also called Frontotemporal Dementia), a terrible disease which causes the frontal lobe of the brain to shrink and degenerate. Our frontal lobe is responsible for various higher-level functions like decision-making, problem-solving, planning, and controlling emotions. Richard passed in 2021 at the age of 67.

After settling Richard's estate, we worked with his widow Karen to write a new financial plan detailing her cash flow, spending needs, and estimating her income tax payable each year for the rest of her life. Karen is collecting pension income from her career with

Alberta Health Services, the survivor benefit on Richard's pensions from the military and from teaching, as well as CPP and OAS from the Federal government. It quickly became apparent that Karen's monthly cash flow exceeded her spending needs, even when we doubled her estimates for monthly discretionary spending and her annual travel budget.

In fact, because of her high pension income, Karen was already experiencing OAS claw back. OAS claw back is effectively a 15% tax on top of a person's regular income tax rate. This problem was only going to become worse for Karen after age 71, when she would be forced to start withdrawing the RRSPs that she and Richard had accumulated in their lifetimes. While Karen and Richard had only a moderate amount of RRSP room each year they worked (because they had pension plans), they had accumulated nearly a quarter of a million dollars in RRSPs on top of their pensions and other savings.

Karen and Richard had raised two boys who were both established in professional careers, and she was debt free. Karen's only spending needs were for day-to-day expenses, fun spending, and the periodic purchase of a new vehicle. Our forward-looking tax projections for Karen illustrated a significant tax bill on the registered assets, both in the form of income taxes and OAS claw back while she was alive, and substantial taxes payable by Karen's estate when she passed.

As a result of these projections, we presented Karen with a proposal that at first glance may be shocking: we suggested she donate all of her RRSPs to charity. Immediately. All $240,000 worth of them.

We had done our financial planning homework and established that Karen was financially stable without this money based on pension income, home equity, and other savings. Furthermore, given the 50% donation tax credit in Alberta and the fact that Karen would only be taxed on the RRSP withdrawals at about a 40% tax rate, Karen would be able to start a Donor Advised Fund with the $240,000 and net $24,000 of tax refunds in the process. Note: to keep the average tax rate down we processed the RRSP withdrawals and the resulting charitable contributions half in 2023 and half in 2024.

Karen agreed to be interviewed for this book. Here are some snippets from that conversation:

How have your motivations or perspectives on charitable giving evolved over the years? *Very much. When I was younger, we were more self-focused. Experiencing life and raising a family gives one a larger perspective, which may be overwhelming, but if you pick a couple of causes and focus on those, I believe it does make a difference.*

What inspired you to become actively involved in philanthropy and contribute significantly to charitable causes? *It was my career in healthcare and seeing difficult situations people could find themselves in, plus Richard's involvement in the Army Reserve.*

Do you involve your family or close associations in your philanthropic activities? *I did talk to the boys, but they did not agree on anything *laughs*. Eventually I decided to move ahead knowing that the charities I selected could be changed in the future.*

What type of impact do you hope to achieve through your philanthropic efforts? *I hope the donations help find better treatments for dementia, and support the afflicted individuals and the families that care for them.*

What do you hope to accomplish by telling your story publicly? *To make other people aware that they can do good things with funds they don't need. This was better than paying more taxes!*

Was there a specific experience or moment that influenced your decision to make a substantial charitable donation? *I was totally unaware that something like this was available until the discussion with you, Hal. I feel fortunate I was able to do it.*

Do you want to share any words about losing Richard early and creating this legacy in your names? *Wow, that's a hard one. Life didn't hand us a very good event; I expected to have a life partner for much longer. I get some comfort knowing that these are the things that represent Richard and Karen's values, and that this charitable legacy will carry on.*

Money, even money used for charitable purposes, cannot replace a lost loved one, but it can create a meaningful legacy. The M. Family Charitable Fund is now donating over $12,000 annually in Richard's memory, supporting the Valour Place Society in Edmonton, the Alzheimer Society of Alberta, and the Hope Mission in Edmonton

Reflection:

Who have you consulted with when consider-ing charitable giving in the past? Why them? Did talking to others affect your thoughts?

21
Case Study

Funding Insurance from Excess Cash Flow in Retirement

"One child, one teacher, one book and one pen can change the world." – Malala Yousafzai

SOMETIMES A RETIRED HOUSEHOLD FINDS THEMSELVES WITH excess retirement cash flow accumulating in their bank account. We see this when someone's combined pension income and investment income exceeds their spending needs. Milestones that trigger this are often when someone starts collecting CPP and/or OAS, or after age 71 when minimum required Registered Retirement Income Fund (RRIF) withdrawals kick in. These types of events generate more taxable income, and while we want all of our clients to have lots of income tax payable as a result of having plentiful income streams, often this means our marginal tax rate creeps into a higher bracket. Rather than paying more tax, our clients often choose to ramp up their planned giving while enjoying the tax credits and the warm heart that come from making the world a better place.

In the chapter *Donate the policy death benefit or donate the policy and the premiums?* we used an example of a young couple with excess cash flow to fund a long-term philanthropic strategy. What if you're 70 and are fortunate enough to have more cash flow than you need now, and your financial planning team has confidently projected that this stability will persist for the rest of your life?

One option was detailed in the chapter *Donating cash from excess cash flow.* Cash donations are versatile, and the commitment is flexible and easy to adjust. But don't dismiss the power of an insurance-based donation strategy as an alternative or a compliment alongside other strategies such as donating from cash flow and options from the chapter *Donations of publicly traded securities.*

In the chapter *Creating a new insurance policy to fund a legacy goal* we used an example for a 60-year-old couple. While someone in their 60s might still be working, as mentioned above we often find that our clients have a lot of extra cash flow in their 70s and beyond, once RRIF minimum withdrawals are triggered. Here's proof that even a septuagenarian couple can consider the insurance option (subject to health underwriting).

Using the same criteria as noted at the end of the chapter *Creating a new insurance policy to fund a legacy goal* (a mixed sex couple of average health), and an insurance policy set up to start with a $250,000 death benefit and a $1000/m premium payment, we come up with approximately:

Policy year	Age of clients	Cumulative premiums paid	Projected death benefit/ donation	Tax credit to final estate	Net spend over time
1	70	$12,000	$250,000	$125,000	-$115,000
5	75	$60,000	$260,000	$130,000	-$70,000
10	80	$120,000	$284,000	$142,000	-$22,000
15	85	$180,000	$324,000	$162,000	$18,000
20	90	$240,000	$370,000	$185,000	$55,000
25	95	$300,000	$422,000	$211,000	$89,000
30	100	$360,000	$466,000	$233,000	$127,000

If both members of the couple pass away in the first decade of having the insurance coverage, the donation tax credit exceeds the amount that they've spent on premiums. According to Stats Canada the average 70-year-old male will live another 13 years, and his 70-year-old female partner will live another 17 years. Those are only averages and overall, there is better than a 25% chance that one of the two will live to be 90 years old.

If both members of the couple pass peacefully in their sleep after their 100th birthday party is over, then they will have spent $360,000 over 30 years to fund a $466,000 charitable donation, while earning a potential tax credit for the final estate of $233,000.

This type of planning must be undertaken carefully, because as noted in the chapter *Giving in Real Life - Give now or later* there is some chance that there is not enough tax payable at death to use such a large tax credit (though as mentioned previously, tax relief is rarely the primary motivation for donating). However, in circumstances such as the family cabin example in *Death and taxes – when you know they're going to arrive at the same time,* or for farmers or small business owners, we can use the donation tax credits when we know the Taxman is going to show up in the same vehicle as the Grim Reaper.

22
GIVING IN REAL LIFE

An Unplanned Insurance Funded Donation: The Dawn B. Memorial Fund

"The best way to find yourself is to lose yourself in the service of others." – Mahatma Gandhi

DAWN AND PETER WERE CLIENTS OF MY firm for years before I took over their file from a retiring advisor, around the turn of the millennium. We're of a similar age, with children of a similar age, and I have enjoyed working with them and their extended families very much.

In 2020 Dawn was diagnosed with colon cancer. This led to several difficult but important conversations that we had not expected to be having in Dawn's early 50s. One of the more difficult conversations centered around a term life insurance policy that was coming up for renewal in the spring of 2021.

Typically, term life insurance is used to cover a set of risks that we expect to be gone at the end of the term period, and this was one of those cases. The insurance we had placed on Dawn a decade ago was no longer needed to protect their mortgage (nearly completely paid off) or the obligations around parenting their daughter (who was now a young adult). Normally we would have told the insurance company that Dawn was going to decline the option to extend the insurance for another 10 years (something that is typically available with term insurance).

Note that this option to extend coverage is always priced much higher than the original policy because (a) the client is 10 years older, and (b) the insurance company does not do a new round of health underwriting on the policy. It's this second feature that factored significantly into Dawn and Peter's situation.

In February of 2021 we had a video call to discuss the insurance, considering Dawn's increasingly poor prognosis. Despite the discomfort Peter and I felt, Dawn was adamant that the insurance should be renewed because it seemed certain that after a few extra months of paying the higher premium, Peter and their daughter would benefit from receiving the insurance death benefit (which is tax free in Canada).

When Dawn passed that fall, I sat with Peter to discuss the idea of a memorial fund for Dawn. This was money that Peter never expected to have, and while no amount of money can replace a loved one, it was important to Peter to find some light in the darkness surrounding losing his wife so young. Peter decided to create the Dawn B. Memorial Fund with a $50,000 donation and has since donated more. Currently Dawn's Fund is donating over $2500 per year in Dawn's name to causes that were important to her.

Receiving the insurance benefit tax free, and making a substantial charitable contribution also had an incredibly positive impact on Peter's tax returns for several years (remember we can carry eligible donations forward to future tax years in cases when the donation tax credits are larger than we need to offset taxes payable in the current tax year).

Peter agreed to be interviewed for this book to have his and Dawn's story told here. Here are some snippets from that conversation:

What do you hope to accomplish by telling your story publicly? *To help someone else who finds themselves in this situation. They don't teach this in school.*

What advice would you offer to others who are considering making substantial charitable donations? *Know what you are capable of and contribute what you can. Work with a good financial advisor so you can assess how large of an amount you can donate without adversely affecting your own financial future.*

What role do you feel individuals have to play in addressing societal issues through philanthropy? *Everyone has a role to play! Anything anyone can do to help is important, nothing is too small.*

Which causes did you choose to support, and how did you select them? *I consulted with close family and chose two charities. The Edmonton Food Bank (Gleaners Association) because Dawn had been active with them in the past, especially when our daughter was in Girl Guides. The second is SCARS. Every animal we've ever gotten has been a rescue.*

Why the Dawn B. Memorial Fund, and not the Dawn and Peter B. Memorial Fund? *This is for Dawn, something that can keep giving in the spirit of who she was. My legacy is her fund. Even if there were no tax benefits, this is a fitting legacy for her.*

The Dawn B. Memorial Fund supports the Edmonton Food Bank and the Second Chance Animal Rescue Society.

Reflection:

If you were to set up an informal board of directors to guide your philanthropic planning, who would you ask to be on the board? What do you hope each person would contribute?

_____

_____

_____

_____

_____

_____

_____

_____

_____

_____

_____

_____

_____

_____

_____

_____

_____

23

Causes That Are Not Eligible Charities

"One small act of kindness can have a ripple effect that reaches far beyond what we can imagine." – Unknown

THERE ARE MANY GREAT CHARITIES TO SUPPORT locally, nationally, and internationally. There are also many great causes to support that don't meet the requirements to become a registered charity in Canada.

GoFundMe and similar online crowdfunding platforms do not qualify for charitable donation receipts. When you donate to a cause that appeals to you, you are essentially gifting cash to the organizer of the campaign. The vast majority of fundraisers have good intentions; however, it is important to protect yourself from fraudulent individuals who may launch fake campaigns or spoof real ones in an effort to get you to contribute to them instead of the intended campaign.

Non-profit (or not-for-profit) organizations are not always eligible for charitable status because they do not fulfill the criteria set by the government which, to review, is that their purpose is:

- The relief of poverty,
- The advancement of education,
- The advancement of religion, or
- Other purposes that benefit the community.

Common examples of non-profits are some social groups, community leagues, sports associations, and festivals. At a glance these may seem to fit the category of "purposes that benefit the community," however it may be hard to argue that a children's sports league benefits the community at large, rather than just the league participants. Hence the organization can operate on a non-profit basis and not be subject to paying taxes, but also not be a registered charity.

Micro-lending organizations, for example Kiva, are not charitable giving organizations because they lend money to recipients with the expectation of repayment. In theory you could set up an account with a micro-lender, deposit some money, lend it out, get paid, and then take your money back. That's not charity, that's a business arrangement. In practice people tend to make new loans after old ones are repaid, but again, each individual transaction is a loan, not a donation.

B Corporations are companies that have gone through a certification process to demonstrate a commitment to corporate accountability and social impact. B Lab, the organization that certifies B Corporations, aims to move our economic system towards a new model that emphasises the interests of all of society, not just profits for the owners/shareholders. The corporations can operate in any sector of the economy, not just the ones that meet the criteria above for being considered an eligible charity.

Before supporting a cause, it is important to understand if it is a registered charity, or an organization working under one of the structures listed above. That may not change your decision to contribute, but it's always important to decide using all of the available information.

24
Case Study

Donating an Inheritance, Then Using Insurance to Create Your Estate

"Charity whispers softly, but its echoes resound loudly." – Maya Kingston

IN THE CHAPTER ON *Purchasing a new insurance policy to fund a legacy goal* we used an example of a 60-year-old couple who were willing to commit to spending $500/month on an insurance policy that would donate exactly $500,000 to charity once they've both passed away. Remember they only have to pay for the policy for 20 years, even if they live long past age 80 the insurance will be in place for the rest of their lives.

Something often happens to 60-something people though: their parents pass away, and they inherit. Imagine this couple inherited some amount of money, and there was at least $500,000 that they were confident (after consulting with their financial planning team) that they would not need to fund their retirement. If they had been considering creating a Donor Advised Fund as part of their estate, they could donate the excess $500,000 right now and bring the DAF into existence immediately!

What effect does that have on their finances?

First, a $500,000 donation would create around $200,000 to $250,000 of tax credits (depending on their province of residence) that can be used over several years to minimize the couple's taxes payable and maximize the benefit from the tax credit. Having the tax credits while they are still alive guarantees we'll be able to make use of the credits.

Second, the DAF starts making donations now, rather than after they've both passed, which is likely to be 20+ years in the future. At a 5% disbursement rate, $25,000 a year starts flowing to the causes that are important to the clients. An extra 20 years of $25,000/year = $500,000 that gets donated before they've passed! Even more if the DAF holds investments that earn at return that is more than the 5% disbursement rate. For example, if we earn 6% and donate 5%, the gradually increasing donations add up to $550,000 over 20 years. After 20 years the DAF still exists (probably with a value of about $610,000) and continues donating indefinitely. See the table at the end of this chapter.

What about the estate they might want to leave to their children (who have just lost their grandparents)?

Remember that before receiving the inheritance, these clients were thinking about committing $500/month to an insurance policy with a $500,000 death benefit. Now that they've already created their DAF, they can still get that policy, and instead make their children the beneficiaries of that money.

But there's more! The value of the donation tax credit on the $500,000 cash donation is about double what it would take to finance the original $500,000 life insurance policy. They could use the money from those tax credits to fund two more policies of the same size and add another $1,000,000 to their estate. The combination of the $500 per month of free cash flow and leveraging the donation tax credits into more life insurance can create an estate payout of $1,500,000!

Let's review.

Basic charitable strategy:

- Commit $500/month out of pocket for insurance.
- Donate $500,000 at death.
- DAF created after death (this adds complexity for the executor).
- $0 to Beneficiary Charities before death.
- Create tax credit of $200,000 to $250,000 for the final estate (which may or may not be completely usable at that time).
- The initial $500,000 inheritance grows to an estimated $1,229,000 (after taxes) for the grandchildren if their parents (the middle generation) pass away in their early 80s.

Advanced charitable strategy:

- Donate $500,000 from the inheritance now.
- Commit $500/month out of pocket for insurance, plus the value of the tax credits on the $500,000 donation.
- DAF created immediately.
- Estimated $610,000 value of DAF at death (age at 80). This amount continues to grow over time.
- Estimated $550,000 disbursed to Beneficiary Charities before death (death at age 80). At age 80 the $610,000 DAF will disburse $30,500, and the annual amount grows over time.
- Large insurance policy creates $1,500,000 estate benefit for family, without investment risk.

A sharp eye will note that the value of the estate these clients will leave for their kids is nearly the same in both cases. In the basic scenario it is the combined value of the donation tax credits at death and the after-tax value of the investment account formed with the $500,000 inheritance. This puts us somewhere in the $1,350,000-$1,500,000 range depending on how much of the tax credits are usable and how the investments perform. In the advanced scenario we lock in a $1,500,000 inheritance for the next generation with no investment risk.

The biggest difference between the two scenarios is the charitable impact. The basic strategy does not create the Donor Advised Fund until after the couple has passed, and the Beneficiary Charities are unlikely to get any donations until two or three years after that (while the estate settles). The advanced strategy creates the DAF immediately and the Beneficiary Charities are helped 20 years sooner, to an estimated cumulative value of $550,000. The numbers could be calculated for deaths at age 85 or 90, and then of course the value of the extra years of donations would be even larger.

If these are charities we care about now, doesn't that imply they could use our support now? See more of this discussion in the chapter *When to give: Now, ongoing, later?*

Effect of starting a $500,000 DAF immediately:

Starting Donation:	$500,000		
Annual Donations:	$0		
Disbursement rate:	5%		
Investment return:	6%		
Year	Starting Balance	Investment Gain	Disbursed to charity	Ending Balance
1	$500,000	$30,000	$25,000	$505,000
2	$505,000	$30,300	$25,250	$510,050
3	$510,050	$30,603	$25,503	$515,151
4	$515,151	$30,909	$25,758	$520,302
5	$520,302	$31,218	$26,015	$525,505
6	$525,505	$31,530	$26,275	$530,760
7	$530,760	$31,846	$26,538	$536,068
8	$536,068	$32,164	$26,803	$541,428
9	$541,428	$32,486	$27,071	$546,843
10	$546,843	$32,811	$27,342	$552,311
11	$552,311	$33,139	$27,616	$557,834
12	$557,834	$33,470	$27,892	$563,413
13	$563,413	$33,805	$28,171	$569,047
14	$569,047	$34,143	$28,452	$574,737
15	$574,737	$34,484	$28,737	$580,484
16	$580,484	$34,829	$29,024	$586,289
17	$586,289	$35,177	$29,314	$592,152
18	$592,152	$35,529	$29,608	$598,074
19	$598,074	$35,884	$29,904	$604,054
20	$604,054	$36,243	$30,203	$610,095
Sum of charitable donations			$550,475	

25

An Excess of Inheritance: The Rudy and Eleonore K Memorial Fund

"Charity is a supreme virtue and the great channel through which the mercy of God is passed on to mankind. It is the virtue that unites men and inspires their noblest efforts." – Conrad Hilton

DIANE HAS BEEN A CLIENT OF MINE for over two decades, having been referred by good friends who were themselves referred to me by other good friends.

Diane's life path never led to children or other financial dependents. She enjoyed a rewarding career in Edmonton as a healthcare professional before retiring at what most of us would consider an early age, having earned a full pension. During our retirement planning conversations Diane indicated that she expected to eventually move to BC to care for her aging parents.

Unfortunately, Diane's parents both passed relatively soon into her retirement. After many trips back and forth to BC to settle her parents' affairs, Diane found herself receiving an inheritance that she did not need to support her own retirement. Discussions with Diane about charitable giving led to the topic of a memorial fund. Charitable giving and a strong sense of faith were hallmarks of Diane's upbringing, so it was a relatively easy decision on Diane's part to move ahead with the creation of a Donor Advised Fund in the name of her parents.

The initial donation to the DAF was made using the money from Diane's inheritance. In addition, Diane has also named the DAF as the beneficiary of her registered retirement accounts, which will more than offset the taxes her estate would be responsible for based on those accounts being taxable when she passes away. Diane has also used her strong cash flow to purchase a small permanent insurance policy that will leave some money to her niece and nephew.

Diane agreed to be interviewed for this book. Here are some snippets from that conversation:

What inspired you to become actively involved in philanthropy and contribute significantly to charitable causes? *It was something I grew up with, something my family has done for generations. There's something good about giving – it reframes the world.*

What influenced your decision to make this substantial charitable donation? *Access to a larger amount of money because of my parents' estate and the desire to continue our family values. When you receive a gift, some of it should be shared with others. All of my wealth and income is not mine; it comes from life and God and part of it needs to be given back as a thank you.*

What do you remember about the approach your family took to giving in your youth? *It was just part of the atmosphere we grew up in.*

It was never appropriate to spend all your earnings. First you saved and donated, then you lived on the remainder.

What do you hope to accomplish by telling your story publicly? *To allow someone else to discover that it's possible for one person to be part of the larger good, that one person can be part of a larger whole that can make a difference.*

What advice would you offer to someone starting on the charitable giving path? *You don't have to start big. Build a small habit and grow from there. Be consistent, giving should not be a one-time event. Be thoughtful in your giving, not emotional based on the most recent cause or tragedy to hit the headlines.*

The Rudy and Eleonore K. Memorial Fund supports the Mennonite Central Committee of Canada.

Reflection:

What role do you think average individuals like you should play in addressing societal issues through philanthropy?

_____

_____

_____

_____

_____

_____

_____

_____

_____

_____

_____

_____

_____

_____

_____

_____

_____

_____

26

Donate via Lump Sums or DAF Distributions?

"The smallest act of kindness is worth more than the grandest intention." – Oscar Wilde

IT IS UNDERSTOOD THAT ANY CHARITY IN the country, or the world for that matter, is grateful for any donations it receives. There are many important causes to support and never enough money. That leads to the question: if we have money to give, isn't it better to give it all now, instead of creating a Donor Advised Fund and gifting a small amount year by year in perpetuity?

The answer depends very much on your personal goals and financial means. If your local YMCA is fundraising to build a new $50 million dollar facility, and you have the capacity to donate $10 million, you have the ability to make a meaningful impact on the campaign (and probably get the building named after you). Maybe your local hospital foundation is fundraising for a new MRI machine, something which costs in the range of $1,000,000. A million-dollar donation is a cheque size that is manageable by a very few wealthy people, well beyond the means of most Canadians.

However, both of these examples have a factor in common: after the big up-front purchase, the organization needs continuous funding to operate the programs at the YMCA or staff the MRI in the hospital. It's quite easy to imagine other situations where ongoing cash flow is essential to maintain the charity's operations: food banks, animal shelters, suicide prevention programs, Doctors Without Borders, etc.

Your philanthropic goals are also contingent upon your personal goals. If you want to create a memorial fund, then it's implied that you want something ongoing to keep that memory alive by giving on an ongoing basis. If you desire to create a family giving fund to teach future generations the importance of giving back, then you need your own legacy giving vehicle. Donor Advised Funds are ideally suited for these tasks.

Any of the strategies in this book that allow us to find or create money to make a charitable donation to a Donor Advised Fund can usually be applied equally well to finding or creating money for a one-time donation directly to a charity.

27

Pension Rich and Child Free: The LouieClaire Fund

"Helping one person may not change the world, but it could change the world for that one person." – Lily Stevens

ANITA HAS BEEN A CLIENT OF MINE since 1997, and she ranks among the most diligent savers I have met during my career. Despite always having a great pension plan, first from the Canadian Armed Forces, and then from the Edmonton Police Service, Anita was always careful to make her maximum allowed TFSA and RRSP contributions, as she constantly worried that she would not have enough money to meet her retirement goals.

Her wife, Lisa, also has an excellent pension from her career as an educator. They are a household with two pensions, two good incomes, excellent savings habits, and no children to rear which makes them unlikely to have any trouble meeting their retirement goals. In fact, our retirement projections showed such a surplus that we projected a final estate well into seven figures. The projections also showed a consistent amount of around one quarter of a million dollars of tax payable in the final estate, regardless of when they pass away.

Anita and Lisa never chose to start a family. If they were to pass away unexpectedly soon, their estate will be split between some of their siblings. If they to live to a ripe old age, then the estate will pass to some nieces and nephews whom they are quite close with. However, in either scenario the projected inheritance values involved were surprisingly large, and Anita and Lisa were open to considering other options.

Anita and Lisa are generous women who had no idea what a Donor Advised Fund was, or how they could use a DAF to create their own private legacy fund. All they had been exposed to in the past was conventional donating; a little here, a little there, plus they consistently sponsor a child overseas. The conversation regarding creating a DAF of their own took place over three meetings spanning almost a year; they wanted to be sure they were proceeding with a complete understanding of the concept, and decisions like this should never be rushed.

These ladies decided to form their Donor Advised Fund and named it after Anita's father and Lisa's mother. They started their DAF with an initial donation of $10,000 (the minimum required amount to create a DAF with our financial firm), and both make automatic monthly contributions to the fund to help it grow. Additionally, they have elected to make the fund the beneficiary of their registered investments which we estimate will eliminate all taxes payable from their estate, while still leaving other money to pass on to family.

Anita and Lisa agreed to be interviewed for this book. Here are some snippets from that conversation:

What inspired you to become actively involved in philanthropy and contribute significantly to charitable causes? **Anita:** *Having you as a financial advisor, reassuring me that I'm okay financially. Asking myself why am I obsessively keeping all this money when I could be doing good with it?* **Lisa:** *110% it's been your example and confidence, Hal. I thought this stuff was for billionaires and celebrities. I'm a teacher and this isn't taught in schools.*

What do you remember about your family's approach to giving in your youth? **Lisa:** *Money was tight, we gave some at the church but mostly gave back through community service.* **Anita:** *There were five kids and one income, so not a lot of extra money. I do remember supporting immigrant families from Vietnam through the church.*

How did you choose which charitable organizations or causes to support? **Anita:** *100% my experience as a police officer and working overseas in the military, seeing where people need help. I knew what causes I wanted to support, and you helped by finding the right charities.* **Lisa:** *It was the conversations you had with Anita and I about what was important to us.*

Did you involve your family or friends in your philanthropic journey? **Anita:** *I told my family, and they loved that our dad's name is in there. They were proud that we were doing this.* **Lisa:** *Ditto for my siblings and having Mom's name in there.*

What do you hope to accomplish by telling your story publicly? **Lisa:** *If you have a good experience, share it so other people can learn. People like us, without all the commas in their bank account balance.*

Have your motivations or perspectives changed over the years? **Anita:** *In the past it was about service and volunteering, but now we have the financial means to give more.*

What advice would you offer to someone starting on the charitable giving path? **Anita:** *If you have the chance and the means,* *don't even think twice. It warms your heart.* **Lisa:** *Find yourself a great financial planning team to see if you can do it.*

What kind of impact do you hope to achieve through your philanthropic efforts? **Anita:** *Reduce pain and suffering in the world.* **Lisa:** *Make at least one day easier for one person or one animal. Hope! It's all about hope.*

The LouieClaire Fund supports Veterinarians Without Borders and international charities that lift women and children out of poverty by providing for basic needs and educational opportunities (Oxfam Canada and Raising the Village).

Reflection:

What role do you think billionaires should play in addressing societal issues through philanthropy?

_____

_____

_____

_____

_____

_____

_____

_____

_____

_____

_____

_____

_____

_____

_____

_____

_____

_____

Effective Altruism

"Effective altruism is about doing the most good you can do, given the resources you have." – Peter Singer

THE EFFECTIVE ALTRUISM (EA) MOVEMENT IS A philosophical and social movement that advocates for using evidence and reason to determine the most effective ways to do good in the world. The movement began in the latter half of the 2000s and the term Effective Altruism was coined in 2011.

EA emphasizes impartiality and the globally equal consideration of interests when choosing beneficiaries; fundamentally the idea that all lives have equal value across the globe. This moves us beyond the "home country bias" that is so apparent in many areas of our lives, towards a more global and humanistic point of view.

The movement's priorities include global health and development, social inequality, and risks to the survival of humanity over the long-term future (including climate change, artificial intelligence, the proliferation of weapons of mass destruction, and pandemics). Some branches of the movement also focus on animal welfare. The idea of Effective Altruism has also been influential in promoting the concept of "cause prioritization," which involves identifying the most effective ways to do good in the world.

The EA movement has been influential in shaping the way people think about charity and philanthropy. It has helped to increase awareness of the fact that some altruistic activities are much more cost-effective than others, in the sense that they do much more good than others per unit of resource expended. Our favourite example is malaria nets. It has been confidently demonstrated that a US$5500 donation to an organization such as the Against Malaria Foundation will purchase enough bed nets to save one life and protect many hundreds of others from serious illness. The Helen Keller International Vitamin A supplementation program has an estimated cost of US$5000 per life saved[10]. Contrast that to the estimated US$50,000 cost of training a single seeing eye dog[11]. From that perspective it becomes difficult to weigh a single person's need for a seeing eye dog over the life of ten people and the health of thousands more.

The EA movement has also been influential in promoting the idea of "earning to give," which involves choosing a high-paying career in order to donate a sizable portion of one's income to effective charities. This is the that path we at Simonson Team Private Wealth Management have chosen, calculating that the time we could spend volunteering for a charity would be better spent working hard at our day jobs, earning more income that can then be donated to effective charities.

The EA movement has been criticized for its focus on measurable impact and its emphasis on quantifiable metrics of effectiveness. Critics argue that this approach ignores the complexity of social problems and the importance of moral values. The movement has

---

10   https://www.givewell.org/charities/top-charities
11   https://www.guidingeyes.org/guide-dogs-101

also been criticized for its strong focus on global poverty, with some arguing that it ignores other prominent issues such as climate change and animal welfare. That said, it is possible to employ the EA approach to evaluating any cause or causes that are important to you.

You can learn more about Effective Altruism at: EffectiveAltruism.Org and TheLifeYouCanSave.Org (plus the book of the same name by Peter Singer). Simonson Team Private Wealth Management uses GiveWell.Org when searching for charities that save the most lives per dollar donated.

Undoubtably there are many causes worth supporting in the world and using an EA lens to examine your approach to giving is just one tool in your philanthropic planning arsenal. Being generous is always better than the alternative, whether it is done from the heart, or using a detailed cost-benefit analysis.

NOTE TO THE READER:

The next four chapters are the advanced topics I warned you about in the preface. If you're not winding up a small business, donating an existing insurance policy, or considering a Charitable Remainder Trust, please feel free to skip ahead to the closing comments.

29

Gifts of Assets that are not Cash or Publicly Traded Securities

"The greatness of a community is most accurately measured by the compassionate actions of its members." – Coretta Scott King

SOMETIMES GENEROUS CANADIANS WANT TO GIFT SOME other type of asset to charity, most commonly real estate, a collectible, or shares in a privately held business. Making donations to charity using assets that are illiquid and difficult to value introduces several layers of complexity to the transaction.

The initial obstacle is the ability, and willingness, of the charity to handle the donation. All charities can easily handle a cash donation, and the vast majority have a brokerage account that can handle the donation of a publicly traded security, but no charity is in the day-to-day business of handling collectible paintings, for example.

The next obstacle is valuation of the gift. A publicly traded security such as stock in a big bank has a clear value based on what the price of the stock is trading at on the public markets the day it is transferred into the charity's brokerage account. Again, using the example of a piece of collectable art, what value can we assign to that? For items valued under $1000, CRA will accept the opinion of a qualified person employed by the charity, but again, how many charities are in the business of collecting art? For items over $1000 in value, CRA will require that a qualified and reputable appraiser provide a formal written appraisal of the collectible in question. Who will pay for the appraisal? If the donor is donating the art because they do not have available cash to donate, then will the charity pay? What if the appraisal reveals a much lower value than the donor led the charity to believe?

The tax treatment of these unique gifts is also different. As we covered in the chapter *Donations and Taxes for Individuals,* donating a publicly traded stock that has increased in value exempts the donor from capital gains taxes on the donation. This tax savings along with the tax credit for the value of the donation combine to have a powerful effect on reducing the out-of-pocket cost to the donor. A donation of a collectible or a piece of property is a deemed disposition by the donor, and CRA will expect income to be reported by the donor. While the income reported will always be the same or less than the value of the donation (the income being the difference between what you paid for it and the appraised value when you donate it), the donor needs to be aware that it is different from donating that big bank stock.

Stock options are an "in between" type of security; not quite a stock, but potentially publicly traded. Employee stock options that are not liquid can be used to finance a donation, but great care must be taken to perform the steps of the donation in the correct sequence and timeframe to minimize any taxable exposure to the donor.

The most complex scenario is probably the donation of shares in a private company, which in some circumstances (when a shareholder donates shares of a company that they or their immediate family control) may not even be allowed. In other circumstances, a sale of the shares needs to be negotiated in advance, with the shareholder donating the shares to a charity which immediately sells them to a third party. Small business donation strategies require careful coordination between your financial/philanthropic advisor, your accountant, and your lawyer.

Covering every possible type of donation is beyond the scope of this short introductory book. Your author again leaves you with the suggestion to seek out formal advice specific to your situation from a financial advisor qualified in the areas of philanthropic and tax planning.

30

Corporate Donations and Taxes

"No one has ever become poor from giving." – Anne Frank

IN THE CHAPTER ON *DONATIONS AND TAXES for Individuals*, we reviewed the difference between tax deductions and credits, and how charitable donations made by individual taxpayers generate credits that reduce taxes payable. In this chapter we detail how charitable donations generate a deduction for corporate taxpayers (versus the tax credits that individuals receive) and compare the tax benefits of personal versus corporate giving.

Donations Give Deductions, Not Credits

Similar to personal donations, deductions arising from charitable donations are limited to 75% of a corporation's net income for a given tax year. Unlike credits, deductions have tax benefits that depend on both the level and composition of a corporation's net income. Starting from the top, the deductions are applied against active business income above the small business limit, then corporate investment income, and finally business income below the small business limit.[12]

Should a Business Owner Make Personal or Corporate Donations?

Differences in provincial tax credits for donations complicate the comparison between someone who can give via their corporation or personally. For simplicity, we assume perfect integration of tax rates, meaning that there is no difference between a shareholder earning an additional $1000 in the form of salary, or via dividends from their small business shares.

To begin, consider the effect of an additional $1000 of business income that is immediately donated. Let's also assume that earlier donations in excess of $200 have been made. As noted above, corporate donations are treated as deductions, so the incremental business income and matching donation cancel each other out.

Now suppose the $1000 in additional business income is paid to the shareholder as salary, and the shareholder makes a matching $1000 donation. As wages are also a corporate deduction, there is no change to the corporation's tax position. As seen below, the shareholder's province of residence determines whether the donation is a net gain or loss[13]:

---

12   The small business limit is $500,000 and, for the purposes of this chapter, corporate investment income always excludes Part IV dividends.
13   See the chapter *Donations and Taxes for Individuals* for detailed information regarding donation tax credits by province.

Province	AB	BC	ON
Incremental Salary	$1000	$1000	$1000
Personal Tax (top bracket)	($480)	($535)	($535)
Donation	($1000)	($1000)	($1000)
Donation Tax Credit	$500	$458	$464
Net Gain (Loss)	$20	($77)	($71)

Based on the 2024 tax rates, the net gain / loss calculation above shows incremental donations are best made personally in Alberta, and corporately in British Columbia and Ontario.

Corporate Donations of Appreciated Securities

While donating appreciated securities instead of cash benefits individual taxpayers (see the chapter *Donations of Publicly Traded Securities*) corporations can also benefit from the creation of a capital dividend account (CDA) balance. The CDA balance represents the amount of dividends that the company can pay out to its shareholders tax-free, which is to say the shareholder receives the dividend without having to report any taxable income.

Consider a corporation that donates securities with a market value of $100 and an original purchase price of $20. Just like an individual, corporations are recognized for a $100 gift with zero taxable capital gains.

What makes the corporate gift more attractive is the increase in the CDA balance. In the example above, the entire capital gain ($100 - $20 = $80) is added to the CDA, making room for tax-free capital dividends. Were the corporation to sell the security and donate cash, the $80 capital gain generates only $40 of CDA balance. As with individual donations, corporate in-kind donations of appreciated securities is the better tax strategy.

Section 85 Applications

Taxpayers who own appreciated securities that they wish to donate may benefit from first transferring them to their corporation. Section 85 of the Income Tax Act provides a mechanism that allows for tax-free transfers to your corporation. Once your corporation owns the securities, an in-kind donation provides the benefits described above, including increases to the CDA.

The taxpayer's province of residence plays a role, as does the availability of liquid assets to pay capital dividends. Finally, as corporations are not subject to alternative minimum tax (AMT) considerations, a transfer and donate in-kind strategy could have additional tax efficiencies. As ever it is essential to discuss these strategies with your accountant and philanthropic planning team so that you can choose the most effective strategy for your situation.

31

Winding Up a Business While Avoiding Triple Taxation (50% capital gains inclusion)

"Compassion is the root of charity."
– Lailah Gifty Akita

Please note that:

1. The tax calculations in this chapter are done based on the 2023 tax year, without the June 2024 proposed change to increase the capital gains inclusion rates for businesses to 66.67% on all gains, and 66.67% for individuals on the amount of their gains over $250,000 (50% for gains up to $250,000). All other details are identical to the following chapter with the 2024 tax year math. Both versions are included because, at the time of writing, the 2024 changes have not been finalized in law, and even if they are finalized in the near future, there is a chance that a change in government could lead to a reversal of the proposed tax increase.

2. This chapter is a composite case study drawing characteristics from several similar cases our team has worked on in the recent past. This case study is more technical than most of the examples in the book. If you're not a small business owner, please feel free to skip this chapter. If you are a small business owner who will one day sell or otherwise windup your business, please consider this another hypothetical example of concepts you should speak to your philanthropic planning team about.

IMAGINE A SMALL ALBERTA BASED BUSINESS RUN by Ms. Businesswoman. She built her company from scratch, so her small business shares have a $0 Adjusted Cost Base (ACB). She is likely a professional (engineer, lawyer, doctor, dentist etc.) who billed through a small company. After 30 years of successful operation, Ms. B. decides it's time to wind up her business and move on to retirement.

During her working career Ms. B. chose to draw dividends from her small business in place of salary, and therefore she has no RRSPs because she never earned the T4 income required to generate RRSP contribution room. She made some non-registered investments early in her career before Tax Free Savings Accounts (TFSAs) existed, and when the capital gains taxation rules were a little more forgiving. Towards the end of her career, she mostly chose to hold investments inside her company to take advantage of the lower income tax rate on small business income. Hence, she has large non-registered capital gains in her own name because she's had those accounts for longer, and proportionately less unrealized gains inside the company.

At the time of retirement her balance sheet was composed of:

- Personal residence $0 (was sold and now she chooses to rent in a senior's complex – proceeds of the sale were used to top up the TFSA and the balance invested in her non-registered account),
- TFSA $150,000,

- Personally held non-registered investments $1,800,000 (ACB $600,000),
- Corporately held non-registered investments of $2,200,000 (ACB $1,600,000), and
- No debts, resulting in net assets of $4,150,000.

Ms. B. is not married (it makes no difference whether she is single or widowed) so in the event of her passing her assets will be inherited by non-spousal beneficiaries, meaning her estate will pay all the taxes due and pass on purely after-tax money to her beneficiaries.

If Ms. B. passed today with no estate planning, her final tax bill is going to look something like this:

- TFSA $150,000:
  - Zero tax payable,
  - **Net from TFSA: $150,000.**

- Personally held non-registered investments:
  - Value $1,800,000 less ACB $600,000 = $1,200,000 unrealized capital gain,
  - 50% of capital gain included in taxable income = $600,000 of taxable income,
  - Estimated personal tax payable of $270,000 (estimating a 45% personal tax rate).
  - **Net from personal investments: $1,530,000.**

- Corporately held investments get taxed three times!!!
  - Tax One – disposing of the company:
    - » Upon her death, Ms. B. is deemed to have sold her small business shares. Since she built the company from scratch her ACB is $0 and its current value is equal to the value of the investments the company owns; $2,200,000,

- » This type of company is not a qualified small business, so there is no lifetime capital gains exemption available, and the entire value of the company is a gain over the original $0 ACB,
- » That equates to a taxable capital gain of $1,100,000 to Ms. B. personally, creating tax payable of $528,000 (based on this income landing almost entirely in the top 48% marginal tax bracket),
- » Note that the company still exists, and the assets are still in the company, it is just that on our death CRA deems that we've disposed of all our assets (in the absence of a qualifying spousal transfer).
- ○ Tax Two – liquidating the company investments:
  - » Ms. B.'s beneficiaries have no use for a company full of investments, they need to get the cash from the corporate investments into their personal names. Therefore, they sell all the investments held by the company to free up cash for distribution to the beneficiaries,
  - » The company's investments are worth $2,200,000 and cost $1,600,000, meaning there is $600,000 of capital gain to pay income on, with 50% of that gain included in the company's taxable income ($300,000),
  - » Since corporations pay roughly 50% tax on investment income this causes $150,000 in taxes payable by the company.
- ○ Tax Three – winding down the company:
  - » Once the investments are sold there will be a large amount of cash held by the company which now needs to be distributed to the beneficiaries. To do that they redeem the shares of the company that they inherited

from Ms. B.'s estate and are deemed to have received a small business dividend equal to that value,

» There is $2,050,000 left in the company after paying the $150,000 owing for Tax Two taxes.

» The $300,000 half of the $600,000 in capital gains that was exempt Tax Two can be distributed to the shareholders without further taxation.

» $1,750,000 in small business dividends will be taxed at approximately 40%, causing <u>$700,000 in taxes payable</u>.

○ **Net from corporate investments: $822,000.**

Tallying all the taxes payable, Ms. B.'s significant net worth of $4,150,000 has been whittled down to $2,502,000 by $1,648,000 in taxes. About 40% of her net worth has been paid to CRA, even after a lifetime of working and paying taxes! If she has more than one beneficiary, then CRA gets a larger share of her wealth than any one person does.

There is a better way! Ms. B. could choose to wrap up her company before she passes away and create a legacy of charitable giving while almost completely eliminating her taxes payable.

First, with the help of an accountant and lawyer Ms. B. will choose to execute a 'corporate pipeline' reorganization strategy. The details of a pipeline are beyond the scope of this book, but simply put she can create a new company to buy her old company, meaning the capital gain that she would experience on her passing will become payable now. However, the new company is formed with an ACB equal to the value of the current company which helps us eliminate taxes payable when she winds up the new company[14].

---

14   It's worth mentioning that various post-mortem strategies can be executed after the company owner's death, however they are complicated, expensive, and require patience and cooperation from the beneficiaries.

At the same time Ms. B. makes a significant donation to a new Donor Advised Fund that she's created with the help of her financial planning team. As she is making a personal donation of publicly traded securities, her capital gains inclusion rate is deemed to be 0%, eliminating personal taxes on the non-registered investments.

After completing these tax planning strategies, Ms. B.'s estate tax projection looks like this:

- TFSA $150,000:
  - Zero tax payable,
  - **Net TFSA: $150,000.**

- Personally held non-registered investments:
  - Value $1,800,000 less ACB $600,000 = $1,200,000 unrealized capital gain,
  - Ms. B. takes $1,200,000 of assets which have been held for a long time and have $900,000 of gain and donates them to her new DAF:
    - » 0% of capital gain included in taxable income = $0 of taxable income,
    - » Personal tax credit of $600,000 created (50% of $1,200,000).
  - She still holds $600,000 of investments with $300,000 in unrealized gain,
    - » On disposition of these assets half of the $600,000 gain is taxable ($300,000). At a 45% tax rate that creates $67,500 in taxes payable.
  - **Net personal investments: $532,500. Personal tax credit $600,000.**

- Corporately held investments (now only taxed twice because of the corporate pipeline reorganization):

- ○ Tax One – disposing of the company:
  - » No change: a capital gain of $1,100,000 to Ms. B. personally, creating <u>tax payable of $528,000</u>,
- ○ Tax Two – liquidating the company investments:
  - » No change: <u>$150,000 in taxes payable</u> by the company.
- ○ Tax Three – winding down the company:
  - » **no tax payable** on drawing the money out of the company into personal name (by either Ms. B. or her beneficiaries) because of the corporate pipeline strategy.
  - » $2,050,000 less an estimated $25,000 in professional costs to execute the strategy = $2,025,000 to draw out.
- ○ **Net value from the corporation: $1,497,000** after taxes and professional costs.

In this scenario the after-tax value of Ms. B.'s estate is $2,779,500, with some significant differences compared to the original case. Her beneficiaries will inherit slightly more than in the initial scenario that had no tax planning (that number was $2,502,000). Of the remaining $1,970,500 of her original net worth, $1,200,000 has gone to start her DAF, $25,000 was spent on the corporate restructuring, and CRA's share of her lifetime wealth has been reduced from $1,708,000 to only $145,500 ($67,500 taxes on personal capital gains + $528,000 taxes from the disposition of company + $150,000 taxes that were paid inside the company, minus the $600,000 charitable donation tax credit).

In short, CRA loses 85% of its 'inheritance', Mrs. B.'s actual beneficiaries get about 10% more, and the Ms. B. Charitable Fund contains $1,200,000 and will soon start disbursing $60,000 annually to support several charities that are close to her heart.

If Ms. B. were willing to see her beneficiaries get a little less (which would still be a lot of money!) she could reduce her net tax bill to $0 by donating more to charity.

In this scenario thoughtful tax, estate, and charitable planning lead to a huge win for charity, while CRA takes over a $1.5 million loss!

32
CASE STUDY

Winding Up a Business While Avoiding Triple Taxation (67% capital gains inclusion)

"When one gives, two get happy." — *Amit Kalantri*

Please note that:

1. The tax calculations in this chapter are done based on the 2024 tax year, including the proposed June 2024 change to increase the capital gains inclusion rates for businesses to 66.67% on all gains, and 66.67% for individuals on the amount of their gains over $250,000 (50% for gains up to $250,000). All other details are identical to the preceding chapter with the 2023 tax year math. Both versions are included because, at the time of writing, the 2024 changes have not been finalized in law, and even if they are finalized in the near future, there is a chance that a change in government could lead to a reversal of the proposed tax increase.

2. This chapter is a composite case study drawing characteristics from several similar cases our team has worked on in the recent past. This case study is more technical than most of the examples in the book. If you're not a small business owner, please feel free to skip this chapter. If you are a small business owner who will one day sell or otherwise windup your business, please consider this another hypothetical example of concepts you should speak to your philanthropic planning team about.

Imagine a small Alberta based business run by Ms. Businesswoman. She built her company from scratch, so her small business shares have a $0 Adjusted Cost Base (ACB). She is likely a professional (engineer, lawyer, doctor, dentist etc.) who billed through a small company. After 30 years of successful operation, Ms. B. decides it's time to wind up her business and move on to retirement.

During her working career Ms. B. chose to draw dividends from her small business in place of salary, and therefore she has no RRSPs because she never earned the T4 income which is required to generate RRSP contribution room. She made some non-registered investments early in her career before Tax Free Savings Accounts (TFSAs) existed, and when the capital gains taxation rules were a little more forgiving. Towards the end of her career, she mostly chose to hold investments inside her company to take advantage of the lower income tax rate on small business income. Hence, she has large non-registered capital gains in her own name because she's had those accounts for longer, and proportionately less unrealized gains inside the company.

At the time of retirement her balance sheet was composed of:

•   Personal residence $0 (was sold and now she chooses to rent in a senior's complex – proceeds of the sale were used to top up the TFSA and the balance invested in her non-registered account),

- TFSA $150,000,
- Personally held non-registered investments $1,800,000 (ACB $600,000),
- Corporately held non-registered investments of $2,200,000 (ACB $1,600,000), and
- No debts, resulting in net assets of $4,150,000

Ms. B. is not married (it makes no difference whether she is single or widowed) so in the event of her passing her assets will be inherited by non-spousal beneficiaries, meaning her estate will pay all the taxes due and pass on purely after-tax money to her beneficiaries.

If Ms. B. passed today with no estate planning, her final tax bill is going to look something like this:

- TFSA $150,000:
  - Zero tax payable,
  - **Net from TFSA: $150,000**.

- Personally held non-registered investments:
  - Value $1,800,000 less ACB $600,000 = $1,200,000 unrealized capital gain,
    - » 50% of the first $250,000 of capital gains is included in taxable income = $125,000 of taxable income,
    - » 66.67% of the remaining $950,000 of capital gains is included in taxable income = $633,333 of taxable income.
  - Estimated personal tax payable of $345,000 (estimating a 45% personal tax rate).
  - **Net from personal investments: $1,455,000.**

- Corporately held investments get taxed three times!!!
  - Tax One – disposing of the company:

» Upon her death, Ms. B. is deemed to have sold her small business shares. Since she built the company from scratch her ACB is $0 and its current value is equal to the value of the investments the company owns; $2,200,000,

» This type of company is not a qualified small business, so there is no lifetime capital gains exemption available, and the entire value of the company is a gain over the original $0 ACB,

» Because Ms. B has already used the first $250,000 of capital gains at the 50% inclusion rate (on her personally held investments), all this gain is included at 66.67% which equates to a capital gain of $1,466,667 to Ms. B. personally, creating tax payable of $704,000 (based on this income landing mostly in the top 48% marginal tax bracket),

» Note that the company still exists, and the assets are still in the company, it is just that on our death CRA deems that we've disposed of all our assets (in the absence of a qualifying spousal transfer).

○ Tax Two – liquidating the company investments:

» Ms. B.'s beneficiaries have no use for a company full of investments, they need to get the cash from the corporate investments into their personal names. Therefore, they sell all the investments held by the company to free up cash for distribution to the beneficiaries,

» The company's investments are worth $2,200,000 and cost $1,600,000, meaning there is $600,000 of capital gain to pay income on, again including 66.67% of the gain in the company's taxable income ($400,000),

- » Since corporations pay roughly 50% tax on investment income this causes <u>$200,000 in taxes payable</u> by the company.
  - ○ Tax Three – winding down the company:
    - » Once the investments are sold there will be a large amount of cash held by the company which now needs to be distributed to the beneficiaries. To do that they redeem the shares of the company that they inherited from Ms. B.'s estate and are deemed to have received a small business dividend equal to that value,
    - » There is $2,000,000 left in the company after paying the $200,000 owing for Tax Two taxes.
    - » The $200,000 portion of $600,000 in capital gains that was exempt Tax Two can be distributed to the shareholders without further taxation.
    - » That leaves $1,800,000 in the company to be disbursed as a small business dividend, which will be taxed at approximately 40%, causing <u>$720,000 in taxes payable</u>.
  - ○ **Net from corporate investments: $576,000.**

Tallying all the taxes payable, Ms. B.'s significant net worth of $4,150,000 has been whittled down to $2,181,000 by $1,969,000 in taxes. Almost 48% of her net worth has been paid to CRA, even after a lifetime of working and paying taxes! If she has more than one beneficiary, then CRA gets a larger share of her wealth than any one person does.

There is a better way! Ms. B. could choose to wrap up her company before she passes away and create a legacy of charitable giving while almost completely eliminating her taxes payable.

First, with the help of an accountant and lawyer Ms. B. will choose to execute a 'corporate pipeline' reorganization strategy. The details of a pipeline are beyond the scope of this book, but simply put she can create a new company to buy her old company, meaning the capital gain that she would experience on her passing will become payable now. However, the new company is formed with an ACB equal to the value of the current company which helps us eliminate taxes payable when she winds up the new company[15].

At the same time Ms. B. makes a significant donation to a new Donor Advised Fund that she's created with the help of her financial planning team. As she is making a personal donation of publicly traded securities, her capital gains inclusion rate is deemed to be 0%, eliminating personal taxes on the non-registered investments.

After completing these tax planning strategies, Ms. B.'s estate tax projection looks like this:

- TFSA $150,000:
  - ○ Zero tax payable,
  - ○ **Net TFSA: $150,000.**

- Personally held non-registered investments:
  - ○ Value $1,800,000 less ACB $600,000 = $1,200,000 unrealized capital gain,
  - ○ Ms. B. takes $1,200,000 of assets which have been held for a long time and have $900,000 of gain and donates them to her new DAF:
    - » 0% of capital gain included in taxable income = $0 of taxable income,
    - » Personal tax credit of $600,000 created (50% of $1,200,000).

---

15   It's worth mentioning that various post-mortem strategies can be executed after the company owner's death, however they are complicated, expensive, and require patience and cooperation from the beneficiaries.

- ○ She still holds $600,000 of investments with $300,000 in unrealized gain,
  - » On disposition of these assets half of the first $250,000 of capital gains is included in taxable income ($125,000), and of the remaining $50,000 two thirds is included in taxable income ($33,333). At a 45% tax rate that creates $71,250 in taxes payable.
  - ○ **Net personal investments: $528,750. Personal tax credit $600,000.**

- Corporately held investments (now only taxed twice because of the corporate pipeline reorganization):
  - ○ Tax One – disposing of the company:
    - » No change: a capital gain of $1,466,667 to Ms. B. personally, creating tax payable of $704,000,
  - ○ Tax Two – liquidating the company investments;
    - » No change: $200,000 in taxes payable by the company.
  - ○ Tax Three – winding down the company:
    - » no tax payable on drawing the money out of the company into personal name (by either Ms. B. or her beneficiaries) because of the corporate pipeline strategy.
    - » $2,000,000 less an estimated $25,000 in professional costs to execute the strategy = $1,975,000 to draw out.
  - ○ **Net value from the corporation: $1,271,000** after taxes and professional costs.

In this scenario the after-tax value of Ms. B.'s estate is $2,549,750, with some significant differences compared to the first case. Her beneficiaries will inherit slightly more than in the initial scenario that had no tax planning (that number was $2,181,000). Of the remaining $2,200,750 of her original net worth, $1,200,000 has gone to start her DAF, $25,000 was spent on the corporate restructuring, and CRA's share of her lifetime wealth has been reduced from $1,969,000 to only $375,250 ($71,250 in taxes on personal capital gains + $704,000 taxes from the disposition of the company + $200,000 that was paid inside the company, minus the $600,000 charitable donation tax credit).

In short, CRA loses 81% of its 'inheritance', Mrs. B.'s actual beneficiaries get about 17% more, and the Ms. B. Charitable Fund contains $1,200,000 and will soon start disbursing $60,000 annually to support several charities that are close to her heart.

If Ms. B. were willing to see her beneficiaries get a little less (which would still be a lot of money!) she could reduce her net tax bill to $0 by donating more to charity.

In this scenario thoughtful tax, estate, and charitable planning lead to a huge win for charity, while CRA takes almost a $1.6 million loss!

33
ADVANCED

Donating an Existing Insurance Policy

"The simplest acts of kindness are by far more powerful than a thousand heads bowing in prayer." – *Mahatma Gandhi*

THE NUMEROUS CONSIDERATIONS REGARDING DONATING AN EXISTING insurance policy make this one of the more complex topics we'll cover in this book, second only to the chapter *Charitable Remainder Trusts*.

An insurance policy is a type of asset that has a value, and therefore can be donated to a charity. The complications surrounding the donation of an insurance policy asset include:

- Assessing if the policy is suitable to be donated,
- Considerations regarding premium payments when the policy is not yet fully paid for,
- Determining the value of the policy,
- Calculating the tax impact to the donor, and

- Finding a Beneficiary Charity that is comfortable working through these complications!

We'll tackle these issues one by one, working in general terms.

Assessing if the policy is suitable to be donated

Life insurance policies can be categorized in several ways, with the simplest being non-permanent or permanent. Non-permanent policies include most term insurance policies, workplace coverage, and creditor insurance. There is little to no value to a charity in owning these types of policies because in the majority of cases the insured person will outlive the policy. Permanent insurance policies, however, are exactly that: able to be kept in place from now until the end of your life, assuring the charity that it will receive the death benefit one day.

Considerations regarding premium payments when the policy is not yet fully paid for

Sometimes we have an insurance policy in place for another financial planning reason (i.e., not for donating) that changes or abates all together. Two examples of this might be insuring a business interest or protecting against expected taxes payable by your estate. In the cases where we were using permanent insurance for protection, it's likely that we've been paying the insurance premium for years and still have some years to go. In these cases, the Beneficiary charity will be reluctant to accept a donation of the insurance policy without a clear plan as to how the remaining premiums will be paid. Some of the potential solutions are:

- The insurance policy donor also donates an annuity to the Beneficiary Charity to cover the remaining premiums, or even just the cash that the charity needs so that it can purchase an annuity.

For a quick review on annuities please see the explanation in the chapter *Donate the policy death benefit or donate the policy and the premiums?*

- The Beneficiary Charity arranges for another donor to take responsibility for the remaining premium payments, again either via cash or the purchase of an annuity, or,
- The Beneficiary Charity decides that it has the resources to pay for the remaining premiums AND that it makes financial sense for the charity to do so.

Determining the value of the policy

If we're going to donate something of value, then we have to know what the value is so that the charity knows how much of a donation receipt to issue. In the case of an insurance donation, we need to know what the Fair Market Value (FMV) of the policy is. Determining the FMV is a complex actuarial calculation that involves a combination of the estimated value of the insurance policy every year in the future multiplied, by the likelihood that you die in each of those years, all brought back to a net present value (NPV). Net present value is approximately how much the future value of the death benefit would be worth to you in cash today. NPV is described in more detail in the chapter on *Charitable Remainder Trusts.*

A credible valuation from a certified actuary is essential for both the donor and the charity in order to justify the donation value in the face of any questions from Canada Revenue Agency.

Calculating the tax impact to the donor

This takes two forms. The simpler calculation is the same as it is for any charitable donation: what impact does the donation have on the donor's income tax payable, with a particular emphasis on making sure that the donor has enough taxes that would otherwise be payable that can now be offset with the charitable donation credits.

The second factor has to do with the disposition of the insurance policy itself. Again, the insurance policy is a type of asset, and if we give the insurance policy to the charity in return for a receipt at Fair Market Value, CRA is going to want to know what the value of the policy was to us. If the FMV is greater than CRA's determination of the policy value, the donor is likely to be exposed to some taxes payable on the transaction.

Section 148(7) of the Income Tax Act (ITA) defines the transfer of the policy at the time of donation to take place at the largest value of:

- The Adjusted Cost Basis (ACB) of the policy (the insurance company can provide this information),
- The FMV of any "consideration" given for the policy (note: when you donate a policy, you are not selling it, so no consideration is exchanged), and
- The policy's value which, for insurance, is defined in the ITA as the Cash Surrender Value (CSV) of the policy.

The FMV of consideration received for the donation of the policy is going to be zero, so we can discard that option as the value of the tax credits from the donation receipt is not "consideration" received.

If the CSV of the policy is less than the ACB, then the ACB is deemed to be the value of the donation. In that case, the value of your taxable gain is the value of the policy (the ACB) less the cost of the policy (by definition the ACB), and therefore there is zero gain.

It's only if the Cash Surrender Value of the policy is greater than its Adjusted Cost Basis that the donor will be exposed to a taxable gain on the donation. The taxes payable on the gain should be weighed against the donation tax credits.

Finding a charity that is comfortable working through these complications!

After reading the first four items above, I am certain that you can appreciate that there are many moving parts involved in repurposing a pre-existing policy compared to creating a new policy specifically for donating (as discussed elsewhere in the book).

Not all charities are going to have the technical competence to understand a transaction like this, the comfort level to proceed with it, and the financial resources to handle the donation.

Not to mention that you as the donor may plan on living another few decades so you need be VERY certain that the beneficiary charity is stable and will exist to collect the proceeds of the policy.

Summary: In practical terms, there are many variations between types of life insurance policies multiplied by the assorted customization each different insurance company might employ to differentiate their product from their competitors. We can't tackle all the scenarios without making this into a technical manual for financial professionals, which is exactly the opposite of what this book is meant to be.

If you have even the slightest idea that you have an insurance policy that may be suitable for donation, please consult with your philanthropic planning team.

34
ADVANCED

Charitable Remainder Trusts

"Always give without remembering and always receive without forgetting." – Brian Tracy

A CHARITABLE REMAINDER TRUST (CRT) IN CANADA is a type of irrevocable trust where you, as the donor, transfer property into the trust while retaining the right to receive income from it during your lifetime. The remainder of the trust's assets are then donated to a registered charity upon your death or after a specified term.

Charitable Remainder Trusts are not specifically defined in the Income Tax Act, however reasonable guidelines exist for them in practice. That said, CRTs are perhaps the most complex gifting strategy available to Canadians and much like the chapter on *Gifts that are not cash or publicly traded securities,* it is not practical to detail every possible scenario where a CRT might work. Instead, let's start with a basic introduction to CRTs and then move onto a simple example.

Here are some key points about CRTs in Canada:

- Assets: Assets are placed into the trust, with varying tax consequences, but are not actually donated to the charity until the trust ends. This could be after a specific amount of time, or once the beneficiary or beneficiaries have passed away and the trust ends.
- Income Interest: The designated beneficiary (which could be you) receives the income generated by the trust's assets for life or a specified term.
- Remainder Interest: The charity receives the remaining assets after the income interest ends.
- Tax Benefits: You get a donation receipt for the present value of the remainder interest at the time of the gift, which can provide significant tax benefits (because you receive the donation receipt now, even though the gift isn't actually made until later).
    - The present value of the gift is not the same as the current value.
    - For example, if we needed $10,000 in 10 years, and knew we could earn 5% in the intervening time, then it would only take about $6139 today (the literal "present" time) to have $10,000 available in 10 years. Therefore, the present value of $10,000 in 10 years is $6139 today.
    - Using those numbers as an example, placing $10,000 of investments in the trust will yield a donation receipt of only $6139, if we expect that the trust will deliver the assets to the charity in 10 years.

- Capital Gains (for the donor): Because a donation is not being made directly to the charity, a transfer of publicly traded securities to the CRT does NOT come with a 0% tax inclusion rate on any capital gains. This is where things start getting extra complex:

- There are some different rules if the CRT is a spousal trust, which can then provide the opportunity for capital gains relief.
- Section 118.1(6) of the *Income Tax Act* allows a donor to choose a value for the property contributed to the trust at any amount between its adjusted cost base (ACB) - or undepreciated capital cost (UCC) if depreciable property is being transferred into the trust - and its actual fair market value. Some intricate tax calculations will come into play here because a higher declared value means a larger donation receipt, but also a larger taxable capital gain. Declaring the lowest value (the lower of ACB and UCC if UCC is applicable) creates the least tax payable, but the smallest donation tax credit.
- The value the donor declares for the assets donated becomes the ACB for the assets within the CRT.

- Capital Gains (for the trust):
  - In Canada capital gains within the Charitable Remainder Trust are taxable (they are not taxed in the U.S.).
  - Income (interest or dividends) is also taxable within a trust, but the point of a CRT is to pay the income out to the designated beneficiaries, in which case the beneficiaries report the taxable income, not the CRT.
  - If the CRT plans to sell the assets donated to purchase different assets, then the value declared by the owner (see the above point on capital gains for the donor) becomes very relevant to the CRT's taxes.

- Irrevocability: CRTs are irrevocable, meaning once you've placed assets into the trust, you cannot change your mind and take the assets back, or change the designated charity.

Setting up a Charitable Remainder Trust involves several steps:

1. Consult with Professionals: Engage your financial planning team, including a financial advisor with knowledge of donation strategies, a tax professional, and an estate planning lawyer. They can help you understand the implications and benefits specific to your situation.

2. Choose the Assets: Decide which assets you want to place in the trust. These can include cash, securities, real estate, or other valuable property. As with other donation strategies, complexity varies from simple (cash), to moderate (listed securities), to complex (real estate).

3. Select the Charity: Choose a registered charity that will receive the remainder interest. Engage the charity early in your planning process to ensure it is both able and interested in entering a CRT arrangement.

4. Draft the Trust Agreement: Work with your lawyer to draft the trust agreement. This document will outline the terms of the trust, including the income beneficiaries, the charity, and the distribution of income and remainder interest. It also crucially appoints the trustees for the trust, who will be responsible for administering the trust, including making investment decisions and ensuring tax returns for the trust are filed annually.

5. Transfer the Assets: Transfer the chosen assets into the trust. This step is crucial as it legally moves the ownership of the assets from you to the trust.

6. Obtain a Donation Receipt: The charity will provide a donation receipt for the present value of the remainder interest, which you can use for tax purposes.

7. Manage the Trust: The trustee (which could be you, another appointed individual, or a corporation that offers trustee services) will manage the trust, ensuring that income is distributed to the beneficiaries and that the remainder interest is eventually transferred to the charity.

8. File Necessary Tax Returns: Ensure that the trust files any required tax returns and complies with all relevant tax laws. The cost of ongoing tax preparation should be considered when evaluating a CRT versus other donation strategies.

Example Scenario

Jane and Robert are an Albertan couple in their seventies who own a portfolio of appreciated securities worth $1 million. Their portfolio is concentrated in blue chip stocks and long-term bonds, yielding an average of 4% in interest and dividends each year. The portfolio also experiences some capital gain as the share prices increase, however a CRT only allows the beneficiaries to receive the income from the portfolio, not the capital gains. Their adjusted cost base for the portfolio is $500,000. They have decided they want to donate to their local hospital because it provided quality care to several of their family members over the years, while retaining the income from the investments over as long as they are alive.

Steps to Implement the Charitable Remainder Trust:

1. Ananysis: Jane and Robert consult with their financial advisor, tax professional, and estate planning lawyer to understand the benefits and implications of setting up a CRT and decide to proceed.

2. Preparation: After selecting a charity and confirming it is interested and able to participate in the CRT arrangement, the appropriate documents are created by the lawyer.

3. Transfer the Securities: They transfer the securities into the CRT. In this scenario the trustee(s) of the CRT determine that the CRT will hold the existing securities. Jane and Robert decide to declare the full $1,000,000 current value of the securities as the value of the donation. That means they will have a realized gain of $500,000 and must include 50% of that ($250,000) in their income.

4. Receive Income: The CRT is set up to pay Jane and Robert the income from the trust annually (about $40,000) an amount that will potentially increase gradually over time.

5. Tax Benefits: Jane and Robert receive a charitable donation receipt for the present value of the remainder interest, which they can use to offset their income taxes. This value is calculated based on their life expectancy and the expected return on the trust's assets. In this case, the advisors decide that a present value of $750,000 is reasonable, and therefore that is the value of their charitable donation. That size of donation is worth $375,000 in donation tax credits, which is more than enough to cover the estimated $120,000 in tax on their $250,000 taxable capital gain, while leaving $255,000 in credits to offset other taxes in the current and future years.

6. Remainder to Charity: Upon the death of the surviving spouse, the remaining assets in the trust are transferred to the hospital foundation, or perhaps a legacy Donor Advised Fund in their names that disburses to the hospital foundation.

Benefits:

- Income Stream: Jane and Robert receive a steady income stream for life.

- Tax Savings: They receive a charitable donation receipt, which will help offset their income taxes payable for several years.
- Charitable Contribution: They support their favorite charity with a significant gift.

Potential drawbacks:

- Complexity and cost: legal and accounting fees will be incurred up front.
- Ongoing costs: the CRT is required to file an income tax return every year, and any costs related to that are deducted from the income paid out to Jane and Robert.
- Irrevocability: in contrast to a Donor Advised Fund, the Beneficiary Charity of a CRT cannot be changed after the trust is created.
- Lower income potential: if the income stream from the trust decreases for any reason, Jane and Robert will not be permitted to draw on the capital to make up the difference.
- Note: for younger clients, the present value of a donation at life expectancy will be much lower than the current value of the assets, potentially eliminating much of the tax benefit from making the donation.

While CRTs can offer privacy and help manage certain assets, they are less common in Canada due to the complexity and limited tax benefits compared to other charitable giving options. Often the charitable goals of the individual/couple/family can be better achieved through a combination of DAFs and well-planned insurance. However, CRTs still have their place in philanthropic planning, especially in the instances where insurance is not an option.

Closing

I WOULD LOVE TO HEAR ABOUT HOW YOU approach giving back and welcome your feedback on this book. You can contact me via book@halsimonson.ca.

Thanks again to Sarah, Scott, and Devon for proofreading this book. Even with all those eyeballs working, we probably missed a few things. If you've spotted an error, please let us know at book@halsimonson.ca and I will gratefully donate $100 to the registered charity of your choice as thanks for your guest editing.

I am a straight, white, cis gendered, physically and mentally healthy male who was born in Canada to a good family. I could hardly have designed a luckier start to life. I feel strongly that this good fortune creates an obligation to give back. To that end, I've set three important goals to achieve before I retire:

1. Facilitate $50,000,000 in charitable donations.
2. Donate $1,000,000 to my own Donor Advised Funds.
3. Give away 10,000 copies of this book so that others can learn how easy it is to *Give Like a Billionaire*.

Thank you for helping me reach my goals.

Hal

If you'd like to know more about the work Simonson Team Private Wealth Management does, you can learn more at:

WWW.HALSIMONSON.CA

We'd love the opportunity to serve you.

We make the world a better place through values based financial planning, sustainable investing, and philanthropic planning.

Thank you for completing *How to Give Like a Billionaire*.

We would love if you could help by posting a review at your book retailer and on the PageMaster Publishing site. It only takes a minute and it would really help others by giving them an idea of your experience.

Thanks!

PM Store Author's QR Code
https://pagemasterpublishing.ca/by/hal-simonson/

To order more copies of this book, find books by other Canadian authors, or make inquiries about publishing your own book, contact PageMaster at:

PageMaster Publication Services Inc.
11340-120 Street, Edmonton, AB T5G 0W5
books@pagemaster.ca
780-425-9303

catalogue and e-commerce store
PageMasterPublishing.ca/Shop